Art in Action

Credits

Cover: Illustration by Judy Sakaguchi.

Illustrations: 37, Richard Carter; 23(r), 89, 90(r), 128, Barbara Hoopes; 131, Christina Brosio.

Publisher's Photos: All photos by Rodney Jones Studios except as credited below. Key: (t) top, (c) center, (b) bottom, (l) left, (r) right.

UNIT 1: Page viii(t), David Muench; viii(br), Image Bank West/Joe Devenney; 1(b), John Tennant; 3(tl), Margot Conte/Animals, Animals; 4(r), Andrew Moore; 7(r), Lee Hanson; 11, Sydney D. Brown; 13(l), Walter Chandoha; 14(r), Myles E. Baker; 15(l), 15(r), Dennis Smith; 19(r), Lee Hanson; 20, 21(l), 21(r), Douglas Mazonowicz/Monkmeyer Press; 30(r), John Tennant.

UNIT 2: Page 34, The Bettmann Archive; 35(t), Douglas Mazonowicz/Monkmeyer Press; 35(b), Giraudon/Art Resource, NY; 36(r), 38(r), Lee Hanson; 40, Joseph Szaszfai; 41(r), Leven Leatherbury; 44(l), Joseph Szaszfai; 50, 51(l), Scala/Art Resource, NY; 52(b), Computer Graphics Laboratory, University of California, San Francisco; 54(l), Scala/Art Resource, NY; 54(r), Kirk Schlea/Berg & Associates; 55(l), Myles E. Baker; 60(l), F.E. Unverhau/Animals, Animals; 63(l), 63(r), 65(r), Lee Hanson.

UNIT 3: Page 68, Image Bank West/Paul Elson; 69(tr), Lee Boltin; 70(r), Lee Hanson; 71(l), 71(r), 71(b), Leven Leatherbury; 72(r), 73(l), Lee Hanson; 76, Scala/Art Resource, NY; 77, Leven Leatherbury; 87(l), 87(r), Courtesy of Virginia Gadzala; 88(l), Martine Franck/Magnum Photos, Inc.; 91, Joseph Szaszfai; 92(l), Douglas Waugh/Peter Arnold, Inc; 92(r), Image Bank West/Kodansha Images; 93(l), Joseph A. DiChello, Jr.; 94, Bob and Ira Spring; 95(l), R.L. Goodard/Berg & Associates; 95(r), Louis Renault/Photo Researchers, Inc.; 96(l), Image Bank West/Francisco Hidalgo; 96(r), Kirk Schlea/Focus West; 97(l), Werner H. Müller/Peter Arnold, Inc.; 97(r), Image Bank West/Kasho Kumagai; 98, Information Service of India; 99(1), LDS Church Graphics Library; 99(r), Edward Jones/Photo Researchers, Inc.; 101, Jules Bucher/Photo Researchers, Inc.

UNIT 4: Page 103(t), Victor Englebert/Photo Researchers, Inc.; 103(b), Jack Riesland/Berg & Associates; 115(r), Lee Hanson; 116(r), Leven Leatherbury; 119(tr), 119(br), Lee Hanson; 124, Three Lions; 134(l), 134(r), Leven Leatherbury; 135(1), J. Scott Lawrence; 135(r), Robert Brenner.

Art in Action

Guy Hubbard
Indiana University

Contributing Educators:
D. Sydney Brown
Lee C. Hanson
Barbara Herberholz

CORONADO PUBLISHERS
San Diego   Orlando   Dallas   Chicago

Copyright © 1987 by Coronado Publishers, Inc.

All rights reserved. No part of this publication may be reproduced or transmitted in any form or by any means, electronic or mechanical, including photocopy, recording, or any information storage and retrieval system, without permission in writing from the publisher.

Requests for permission to make copies of any part of the work should be mailed to: Permissions, Coronado Publishers, Inc., 1250 Sixth Avenue, San Diego, CA 92101

Printed in the United States of America ISBN 0-15-770054-2(6)
901 062 9876543

Table of Contents

Unit 1   Looking at Art   1

    1   Drawing Lines and Textures   2
    2   Contour Drawing   4
    3   Drawing Mass and Line   6
    4   Value Scale: A Study of Light and Dark   8
    5   Composing with a Viewfinder   10
    6   Beginning with Basic Shapes   12
    7   Careers: What Do Artists Do?   14
    8   Drawing: Adding to an Object   16
    9   An Animal Sketch   18
   10   Painting with Earth Colors   20
   11   Tints, Shades, and Tones   22
   12   Imagining a Fantasy Tree   24
   13   Oriental Art Designs   26
   14   Printing with Natural Objects   28
   15   Kinetic Art: Art That Moves   30
       Exploring Art: Portraits and Biographies   32
       Review: Using What You Have Learned   33

Unit 2   Exploring Art Elements   34

   16   Complementary Color Changes   36
   17   Color Relationships   38
   18   Impressionism: Arranging Dots and Dabs of Color   40
   19   Paint to Music   42
   20   Watercolor Techniques   44
   21   A Watercolor Waterscape   46
   22   Above the Blue Horizon   48
   23   Art Styles of the Renaissance   50

24	Round Art Designs	52
25	Medal and Pendant Sculpture	54
26	Painting Focus: Realism	56
27	Animal Portraits	58
28	From Realism to Abstraction	60
29	Two-View Portraits	62
30	Imaginary Beasts	64
	Exploring Art: A Mythical Zoo	66
	Review: Using What You Have Learned	67

Unit 3 Living with Art 68

31	The Art of Appliqué	70
32	Circular Weaving	72
33	Bark Cloth Designs	74
34	Mosaic Art	76
35	Container Designs	78
36	Coil Pottery	80
37	The Human Figure in Action	82
38	Relief Sculpture	84
39	Costume Design	86
40	Puppets at Play	88
41	Exteriors: One Point Perspective	90
42	Foil Relief Houses	92
43	Greek and Roman Architecture Styles	94
44	Towers and Turrets	96
45	Monuments of the World	98
	Exploring Art: Who Lived in This Place?	100
	Review: Using What You Have Learned	101

Unit 4 Communicating Through Art 102

46	Original Banners	104
47	A Monochrome Self-Portrait	106
48	A Personal Treasure Box	108
49	Transformations and Illusions	110
50	Adventures in Perception	112

51	Surrealism: A Dream Landscape	114
52	Positive and Negative Space	116
53	Styles of Printmaking	118
54	An Illustrated Alphabet	120
55	Graphic Design with Labels	122
56	Greeting Card Designs	124
57	Poem Illustrations	126
58	Technical Drawing and Process Illustration	128
59	Cartoon Art	130
60	Art on Film	132
	Exploring Art: Showing Art	134
	Review: Using What You Have Learned	135

Glossary	136
Artists' Reference	144
Index	146

Unit 1

Looking at Art

Do two people looking at the same object see the same thing? It may surprise you to learn the answer is no. Because we have different experiences, thoughts, feelings, and memories, each of us sees our world differently. The eye can be trained to look for and notice certain things, however.

In this unit, you will increase your awareness of **line**, **shape**, **texture**, **color**, **value**, and **space** by observing and studying the works of master artists and creating your own works.

By studying these **elements of design**, you will be able to identify them in both works of art and in nature. The way a surface looks or feels is called texture. Which of these pictures shows texture? Shapes are flat and have height and width but not depth. Shapes that are repeated form **patterns**. Which picture shows an example of pattern? Curved or similar lines that are repeated show **rhythm**. Which picture here shows rhythm?

Egypt, Figure of hippopotamus *(left side), XII Dynasty (c. 1991-1786 B.C.), faience, 4³⁄₁₀" x 7⁴⁄₅". The Metropolitan Museum of Art, Gift of Edward S. Harkness, 1917.*

The vibrant blue color of "William," a hippopotamus sculpture found in an Egyptian tomb, has lasted more than three thousand years. Variations in lightness and darkness of color are called values. Does William have a lighter value or a darker value? Sculpture is an example of form because it has height, width, and depth.

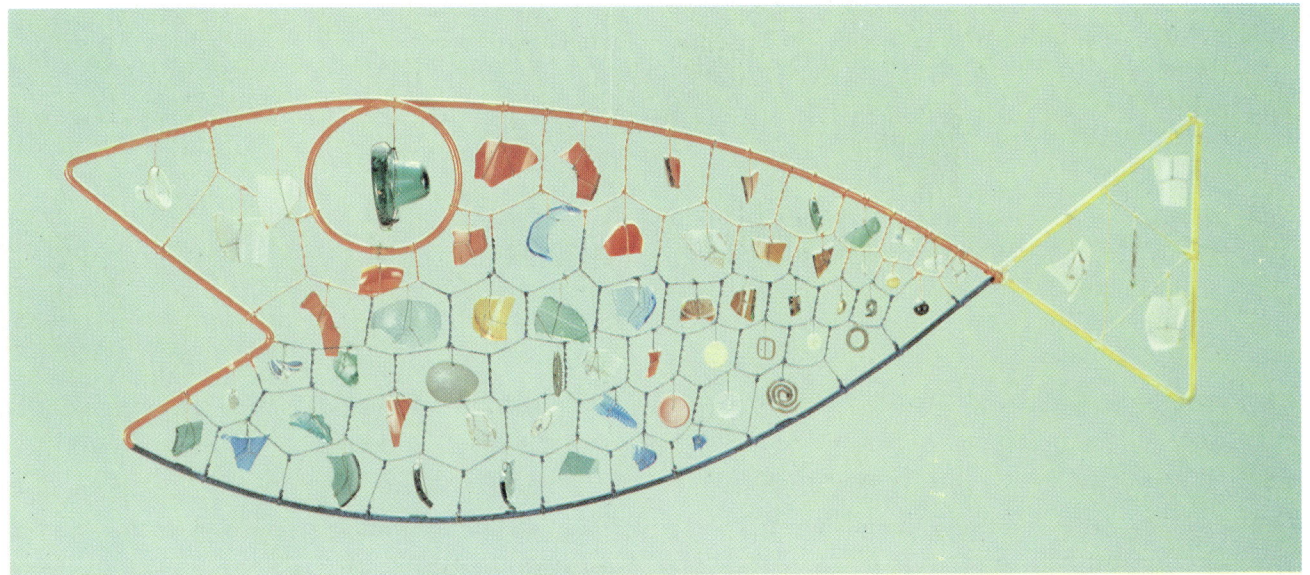

Alexander Calder, Fish Mobile, 1940. Glass, metal wire, and cord, 16¼" x 46 x 3". Hirshhorn Museum and Sculpture Garden, Smithsonian Institution.

The bright, playful fish mobile by Alexander Calder represents space. What other elements of design can you find in this work? This art form also shows **movement**.

In this course you will be introduced to the elements of design in paintings, photographs, sculpture, mobiles, prints, and other art forms.

1 Drawing Lines and Textures

Observing and Thinking Creatively

The drawing of the rhinoceros below was done by an artist who had never actually observed such an animal. Albrecht Dürer, a German painter, printmaker, and draftsman, created *Rhinoceros* in 1515 from a sketch and a description.

Observe the detailed, technical approach Dürer used to outline the main **shapes** of the animal. His use of **shading** and **line** gives the coat of the rhinoceros the appearance of metal armor. By repeating the scalelike shapes on the legs, Dürer showed the **texture** of the hide and also created a **pattern**. What other shapes are repeated in this drawing?

Compare Dürer's drawing with the photograph of a rhinoceros. Look carefully at the shapes of the feet, ears, legs, head, and armor. Which parts of the drawing are **realistic**? Which parts did Dürer create from his interpretation of the description?

In this lesson, you will describe an animal to a classmate, and you will make a detailed drawing from a classmate's description of a different animal. You will increase your awareness of details, and you will experiment with a variety of lines in showing textures and details on your drawing of an animal.

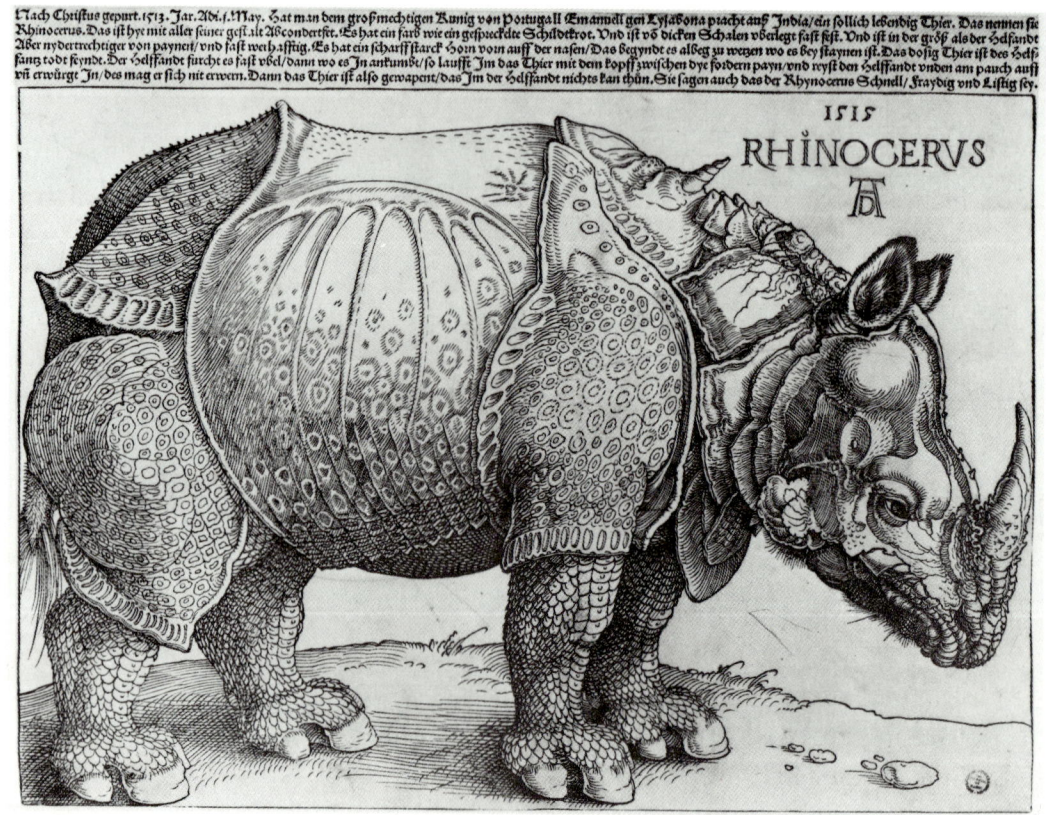

Albrecht Dürer, Rhinoceros, National Gallery of Art, Washington; Rosenwald Collection.

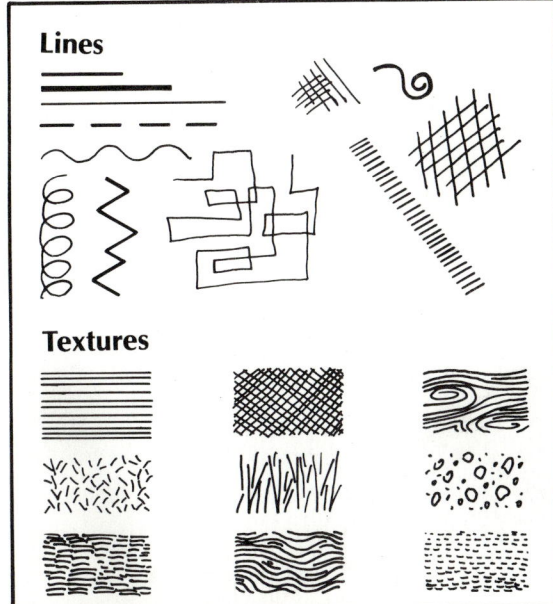

Instructions for Creating Art

1. First, practice making the lines and textures shown in this lesson. Make lines that are curved and flowing, and others that are straight and bold. Experiment with many different kinds of lines, and make several examples of each type.

2. Next, practice showing textures in a variety of ways, using the examples in the lesson. Observe how Dürer showed texture in *Rhinoceros*, and practice some of his techniques.

3. Next, choose a partner and decide who will describe an animal first and who will draw first. Look through encyclopedias or nature books for unusual or exotic animals. When you describe an animal, give very specific and detailed information about the animal's size, ear and nose shapes, length and type of hair, and so on.

4. Have your partner describe a different animal for you to draw. Be sure to use a variety of lines to create the textures in your drawing.

Art Materials	
Pencil and eraser	Paper

Learning Outcomes

1. Point out three examples of textures in your drawing.

2. Describe parts of your drawing where you created a pattern by repeating shapes or lines.

3. Tell what you learned about translating words into images.

2 Contour Drawing

Observing and Thinking Creatively

Can you imagine what things would be like if there were no **textures** or **colors**, only **lines** and **shapes**? The world would be very different without roughness and smoothness, brightness and darkness, or hardness and softness. When a person draws, however, one of the best ways to begin is by looking first at **contours**, or edges and outlines.

When Swiss painter Paul Klee taught art in Germany, he told his students, "Take a walk with a line." He wanted them to explore what could be done with just a simple line. And that's just what Alexander Calder seemed to do in his line drawing of a camel. Notice the playful feeling of this drawing. Calder allowed the line to ramble as it revealed the basic shape of the camel.

Donald Sultan's clean, precise drawing of a lemon reveals only its barest outline. The crisp simplicity of line demonstrates his great drawing skill and control.

Lines can reveal moods and ideas. A thick, heavy line is much more **emphatic** than a thin, light line. If you examine an object closely, you may be surprised at all the hidden lines you find.

In this lesson, you will make a **contour drawing**, a drawing of an object using one continuous line to show outline and details. Contour drawing requires concentration and should be done slowly and deliberately as you observe and draw. You will not look at your paper as you draw; your brain will guide your hand as you look at the object.

Alexander Calder, Calder's Animals, 1931, drawings for Aesop's Fables. Rare Books and Manuscripts Division; The New York Public Library; Astor, Lenox and Tilden Foundations.

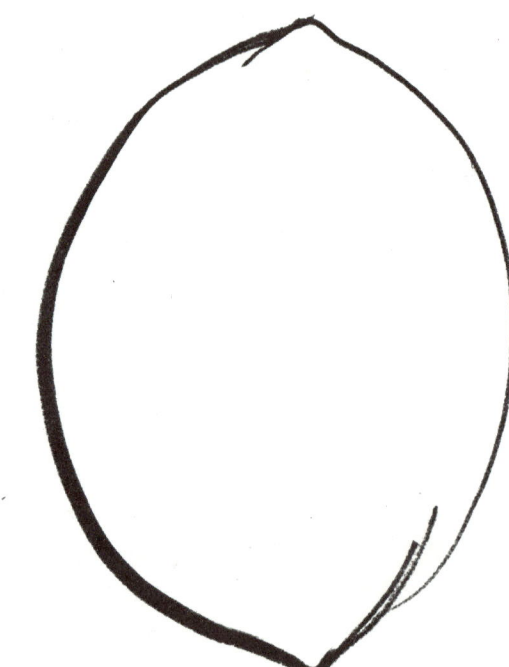

Donald Sultan, Lemon, Jan. 17, 1984, charcoal on paper, 17⅝" × 19¹³⁄₁₆". Blum Helman Gallery, Inc.

Instructions for Creating Art

1. Make a paper "mask" with a piece of paper large enough to cover your hand. Carefully punch a hole in the center and slide the paper halfway down your pen. As you hold your pen beneath the paper, you will not be able to watch yourself draw.

2. Place an object before you and observe it carefully. Slowly draw the outlines of the object. Let your hand move on the paper at the same pace your eye moves over the object as you draw each contour, curve, and edge. It is expected that some of your lines will overlap other lines.

3. Now remove the mask from your pen and look at your drawing. It will show the basic shapes of the object, and because the lines ramble, it may appear messy to you. But doing a blind contour drawing will help you improve your next drawing.

4. This time, draw the object's outlines without using the paper mask. Draw slowly and carefully, and look at both the object and your drawing.

5. When your second drawing is complete, compare the two drawings. Which has more accuracy? Which best captures the feeling of the object?

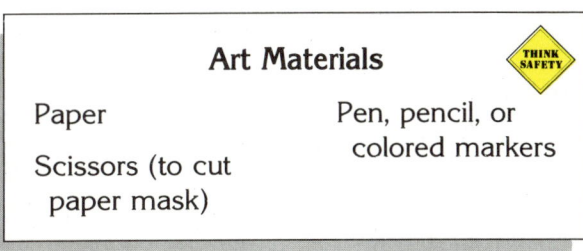

Art Materials	
Paper	Pen, pencil, or colored markers
Scissors (to cut paper mask)	

Learning Outcomes

1. What is a *contour drawing*?

2. How did doing a blind contour drawing help you make your second drawing?

3. Which parts of each of your drawings turned out best?

3 Drawing Mass and Line

Observing and Thinking Creatively

In Lesson 2, you used lines to show the edges of an object in a **contour drawing**. In this lesson, Picasso's drawing of *Mother and Child* is another example of a contour drawing. This great Spanish-born artist had the ability to show beauty, mood, and skill with a few carefully drawn lines.

Look at the mother's right hand in the drawing by Picasso. Run your finger around the contour line. Did your finger come back to the starting point? When lines go completely around an object, the enclosed area is called a **closed shape**.

Now look at the mother's face. If you run your finger around the contour line here, you will not end up where you started. When a line does not connect, the partly enclosed area is called an **open shape**.

How many open and closed shapes can you find in the painting of circus elephants by John Marin? The shapes are filled with color. The area of matter or material inside a shape is called **mass**. What color did Marin use to show the elephants' mass?

In some drawings, artists do not put anything inside their contour lines. Then we say they have **empty shapes**. But Picasso filled his shapes. What colors did he use to show mass in *Mother and Child*?

In this lesson, you will show mass and contour lines in a drawing you make from looking at a real object.

John Marin, Circus Elephants, 1941. Crayon and wash, 19" × 24¾". Courtesy of The Art Institute of Chicago, Collection of Alfred Stieglitz and Robert A. Waller, 49.609.

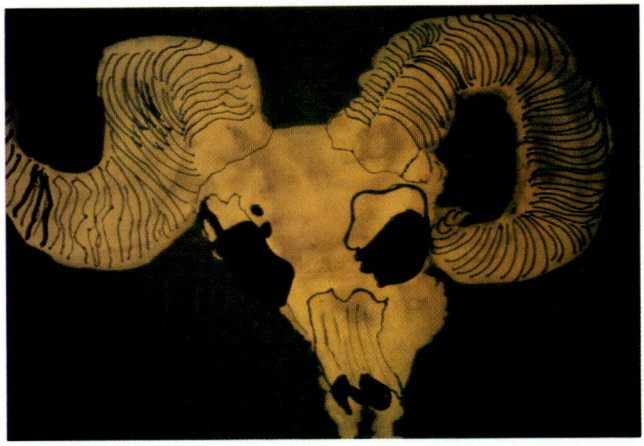

Pablo Picasso, Mother and Child, 1922. Oil on canvas, 39⅜" × 31⅞". The Cone Collection, Formed by Dr. Claribel Cone and Miss Etta Cone of Baltimore, Maryland, BMA 1950.279.

Instructions for Creating Art

1. Find something interesting to draw. It can be an object, like a shell or a tree, or it can be a person who is willing to model for you. Study your subject carefully.

2. *Warning:* be very careful as you work with bleach. Bleach is very harmful if it gets in your eyes. If this happens, *wash eyes immediately* with clear water and go to your school nurse. If bleach gets on your clothes, it will permanently remove color. Use only a small amount contained in a bottle cap. Dip the cotton swab into the bleach and use it like a paintbrush to draw on colored construction paper. Use the side of the swab in broad, solid strokes everywhere that you want to show mass. Let the paper dry. You may use paint instead of bleach if you prefer. If you do, be sure to let the paint dry thoroughly before proceeding to the next step.

3. Use a felt-tip pen to draw the object. You do not have to follow the edges of the bleach shape. Look at the object carefully and draw the edges of what you see, even if they do not match the bleached areas. Finally, use your pen to add details to the inside of the shape.

Art Materials

Colored construction paper

Bleach

Cotton swab

Small bottle cap (for bleach)

Plastic lid

Black felt-tip marker

Newspaper (to cover work area)

Learning Outcomes

1. Explain the differences between *open* and *closed* shapes, and point out examples in the pictures shown here.

2. How did you show *mass* in the picture you created?

3. Tell how the two art pieces shown here are similar and how they are different.

4 Value Scale: A Study of Light and Dark

Observing and Thinking Creatively

Light and dark is not a simple matter of black and white. There are countless shades or **values** in between. The gradual change from dark to light is called **gradation**. Artists use gradation to make objects appear **three-dimensional**—to have **height**, **width**, and **depth**. The part of an object closest to the light source has the lightest value, and the parts farther away have darker values.

Look at the artwork in this lesson. Observe how Allston used gradual changes in shade, or value, to show roundness and depth in the fingers of *Belshazzar's Left Hand.* If there were no variations in shade, the hand would look very flat. Notice the technique Allston has used to give depth to the folds he has drawn.

Allston drew this picture with black and white chalk. The bone structure of Belshazzar's hand is accented by the use of light values next to dark. What effect is created by the use of white?

In this lesson, you will create a value scale and a drawing that shows different values of an object. This exercise will help you become more aware of the variety of shades that can be used in drawing to show roundness, depth, and texture.

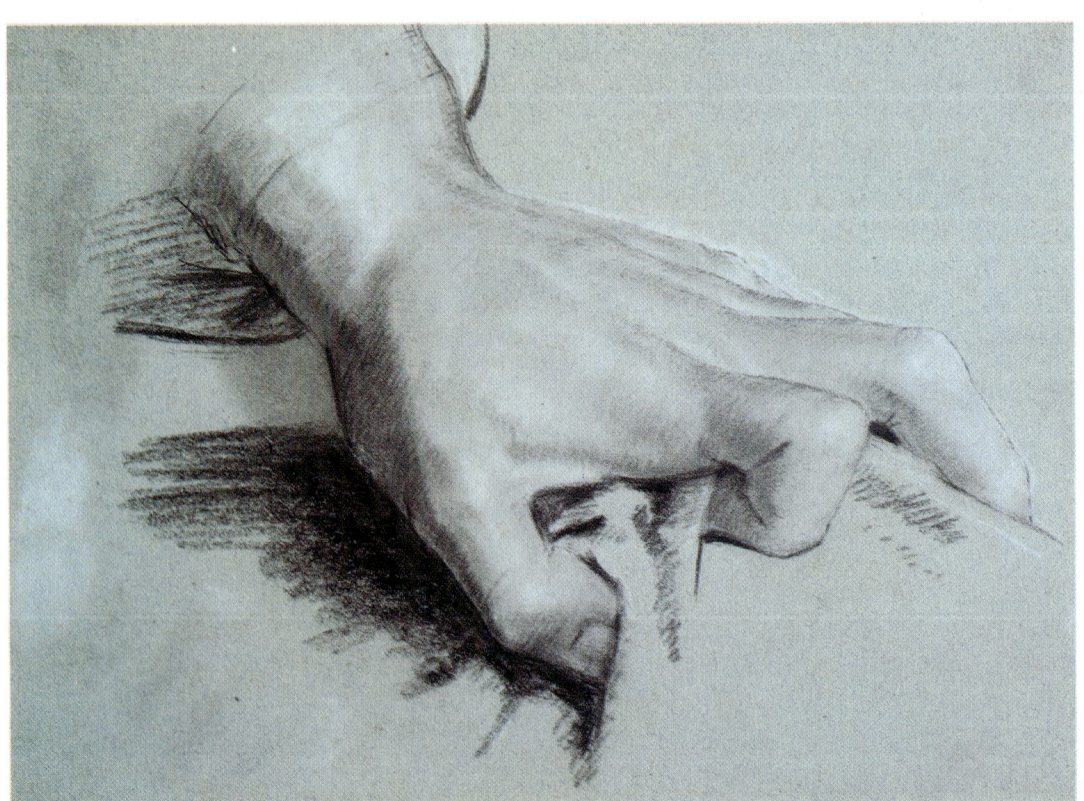

Washington Allston, Belshazzar's Left Hand, 19th century, drawing, black and white chalk on faded blue paper, 9 ¾" × 12 ½". Courtesy of the Fogg Art Museum, Harvard University. On Loan from the Washington Allston Trust.

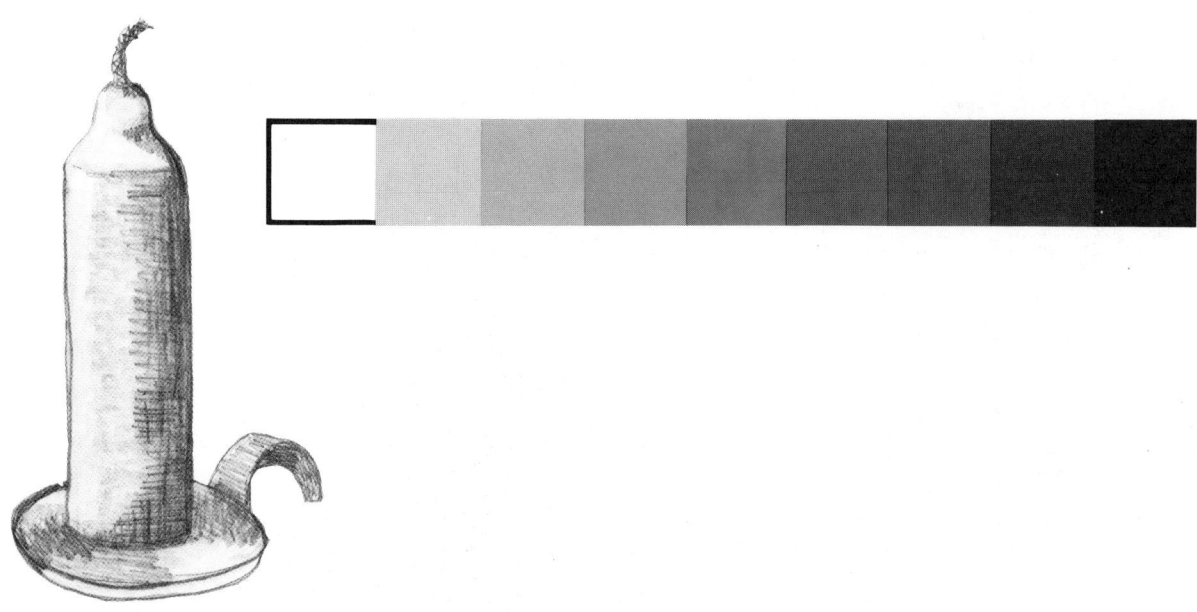

Instructions for Creating Art

1. Divide a piece of white paper with lines to make nine 1"×4" rectangles.

2. Label the rectangles off to the side from the top down in the following order: white, high light, light, low light, medium, high dark, dark, low dark, and black.

3. You may use a soft pencil or charcoal to make your value scale. Begin shading from the middle rectangle, rather than from the top down. This helps prevent duplication of values or arriving at black at the seventh or eighth rectangle.

4. Now use the side of your pencil to shade the bottom black rectangle a very dark, solid black. Then fill in medium, the light and dark, and finally the remaining four rectangles.

5. Remember that it is easier to make an area darker than lighter. However, if you must lighten an area, don't erase. Instead, use your eraser like a sponge and press down and lift off some of the value. If the area is left spotty, pencil it in evenly.

6. Except for white, each rectangle should be filled in evenly. For darker areas, use your pencil to go over and over the area until you reach the right value. Hold the paper up to the light to see if the values change at even rates.

7. Now choose an object with round contours and draw it. Carefully shade in the dark and light areas so that the roundness is shown.

Art Materials

9" × 12" white paper

Cover sheet

Pencil or charcoal and eraser

Learning Outcomes

1. What is *gradation*?

2. How do artists use values to create a sense of three-dimensions in drawings and paintings?

3. What part of your shaded object was most difficult to create? Why?

5 Composing with a Viewfinder

Observing and Thinking Creatively

One of the first things an artist must decide is what part of a scene to draw. Some artists draw pictures from their imagination, and others draw what they actually observe. Thomas Gainsborough, an English **landscape** and **portrait** artist, set up some of his landscape paintings in an unusual way. First, he arranged chunks of coal and broken glass on a table to represent hills, trees, and other objects. Then he moved the coal and glass around until the arrangement, or **composition**, was **balanced**. Finally, using his imagination, he painted the landscape.

A commonly used **rule of compensation** may be helpful in balancing compositions. The bigger the **mass**, the more it should go toward the center. The smaller the mass, the more it should go toward the edge.

When you look at a scene, you are not as free to move objects around as Gainsborough did. But you can choose the view you want to paint. You may show a scene in a tall, **vertical** picture, a square frame, or a wide, **horizontal** view. A **viewfinder** can help you examine different views of a scene and choose the one you like best.

In this lesson, you will make a viewfinder and use it to draw two different views of the same scene.

Thomas Gainsborough, British, 1727–1788, Landscape with a Bridge, c. 1785. Oil on linen canvas, 44½" × 52½". National Gallery of Art, Washington, Andrew W. Mellon Collection.

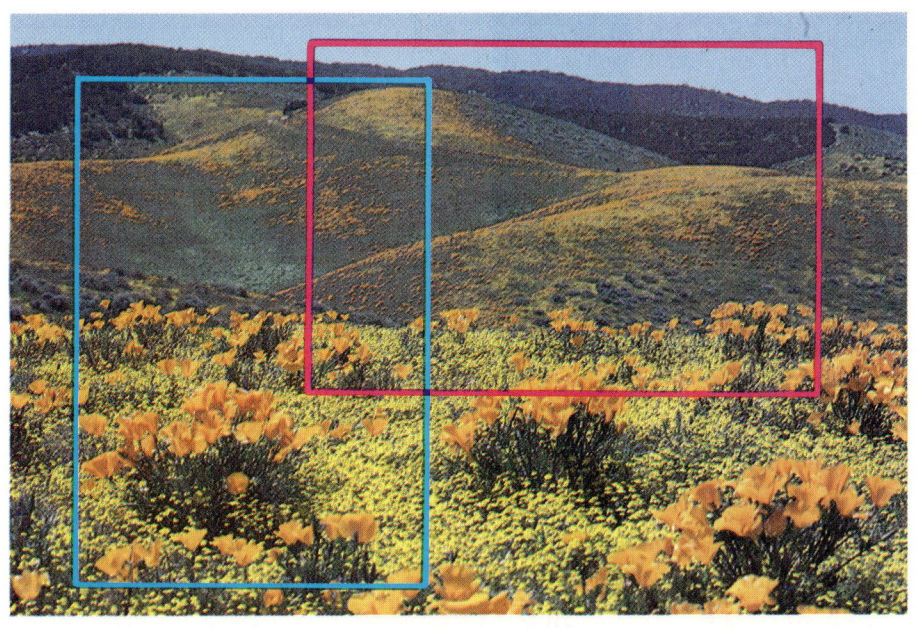
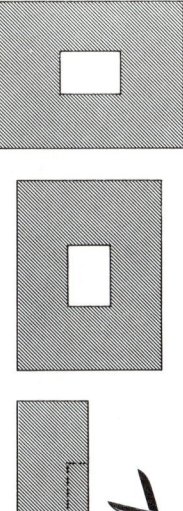

Instructions for Creating Art

1. Fold a piece of paper or stiff cardboard in half and cut out a rectangle along the fold. Open the paper and use the window to look at different views of one scene.

2. Look at the two views of the photograph on this page. How are they different? How are they alike?

3. Now, look for an interesting group of objects around your classroom. Experiment with looking through your viewfinder until what you see makes an interesting composition. When you have discovered two views of the same scene that you like, you are ready to draw your pictures.

4. Using a pencil, pen, or colored marker, draw the large shapes of the scene you are looking at through the viewfinder. Which part of the scene do you want to make most important? Make that part larger or place it in the **foreground**, or front, of your picture. Fill the whole sheet with your drawing.

5. Next, draw in the important details of your scene. You may emphasize a **center of interest** by making one part of your picture larger, more detailed, or more brightly colored than other parts.

6. When you have completed your first drawing, draw another view of the same scene on another sheet of paper. Does your second picture have the same center of interest as the first drawing? Which view do you prefer?

Art Materials

Heavy paper or thin cardboard	Scissors
Pencil, pen, or colored marker	Eraser
	Drawing paper

Learning Outcomes

1. What does *composition* mean in art?
2. How did you show the *center of interest* in each of your drawings?
3. Explain how you could tell you had found a good view in your *viewfinder*.

6 Beginning with Basic Shapes

Observing and Thinking Creatively

Can you explain the difference between a **triangle** and a **pyramid**? A triangle is an example of a **shape**. It is flat and **two-dimensional**—it has **height** and **width**, but not **depth**. A pyramid is a **form**. It is **three-dimensional** because it has depth.

There are shapes and forms all around us, in the food we eat, the furniture we live with, and in the outdoors. Almost all things are made up of four basic shapes: the **circle**, **triangle**, **square**, and **rectangle**. How many of these shapes can you identify as you look around your classroom?

Henri Rousseau (Ru-sō) was a French artist whose work is often called "primitive." His imaginative use of exotic colors and ideas gives his works a mysterious, dreamlike quality. Look at *The Sleeping Gypsy* below. How many circle shapes can you find? See how many other shapes you can identify in this painting.

Notice how shapes and variations of shapes—for example, **oblongs** and **ovals**—create objects in this painting. By repeating shapes, Rousseau creates **patterns** and brings a sense of **unity** to his work.

In this lesson, you will make a drawing using only basic shapes. Then you will make a more realistic drawing of the same objects by softening the lines connecting the shapes.

Henri Rousseau, *The Sleeping Gypsy*, 1897, oil on canvas, 51" × 6'7". Collection, The Museum of Modern Art, New York. Gift of Mrs. Simon Guggenheim.

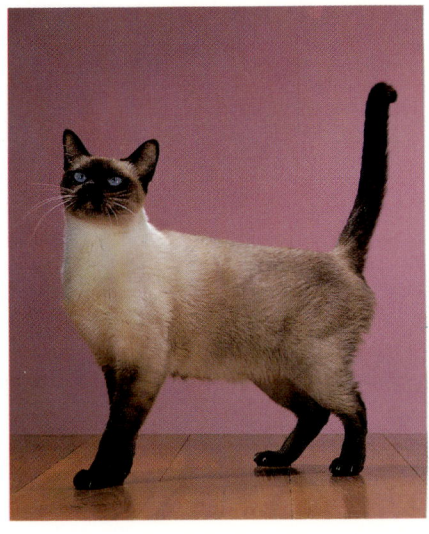

Instructions for Creating Art

1. Look through magazines for pictures of objects made up of several shapes. Practice identifying shapes in different objects. If possible, observe the shapes of animals in a zoo or natural history museum. Then choose an object you would like to draw.

2. Fold a large sheet of paper in half, with the crease down the middle. Now, using only the four basic shapes, draw the object you chose on one side of the paper. Add details to your object, but use only circles, squares, rectangles, and triangles.

3. When you have drawn the basic shapes of your object, you are ready to make a finished drawing on the other side of your paper. Draw the basic shapes again, but soften the edges and add connecting lines where necessary. Change the circles to oblongs or adjust them in other ways to make your drawing look as much like the object as possible. Do not add details that are not in your first picture.

4. When your drawing is complete, compare the two pictures. Can you still identify the basic shapes hidden in your second picture? Did your first drawing help make your second drawing look more realistic?

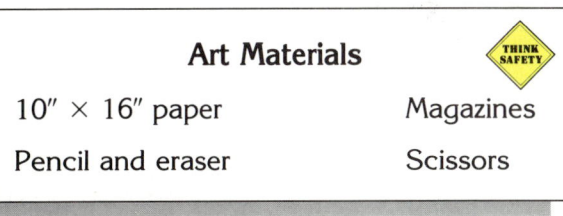

Art Materials	
10″ × 16″ paper	Magazines
Pencil and eraser	Scissors

Learning Outcomes

1. Name the four basic shapes, and explain the difference between a **shape** and a **form**. Give an example of each.

2. Which shapes did you use most often in your drawing?

3. Explain how identifying the shapes in your object helped you make a better second drawing.

7 Careers: What Do Artists Do?

Observing and Thinking Creatively

What must a person do to be considered an artist? It has been said that everyone who creates an original design for anything used by man is an artist. **Design** refers to the way the artist organizes **line**, **shape** and **form**, **texture**, **color**, **value**, and **space** in an artwork.

How many kinds of artists can you name?

Did you include architects, fashion designers, glass blowers, and furniture designers? Don't forget rug makers, color consultants, cartoonists, musicians, jewelry designers, portrait painters, graphic designers, automobile designers, weavers, textile designers, and ceramists. Can you add more to this list?

There are metal sculptors, city planners, interior decorators, art teachers, sign painters, advertising designers, printmakers, and photographers. Do you know what a *lapidary* artist does? This type of artist cuts, polishes, and engraves precious stones. He or she may work for a jeweler.

How different would your life be without these artists? Do you realize that without a printmaker, there would be no paper money? Artists contribute in many hidden ways to help make our lives more enjoyable. In this lesson, you will make a **collage** of the great variety of things artists produce.

Jan Vermeer, The Artist in His Studio, *Kunsthistorisches Museum, Vienna, Austria.*

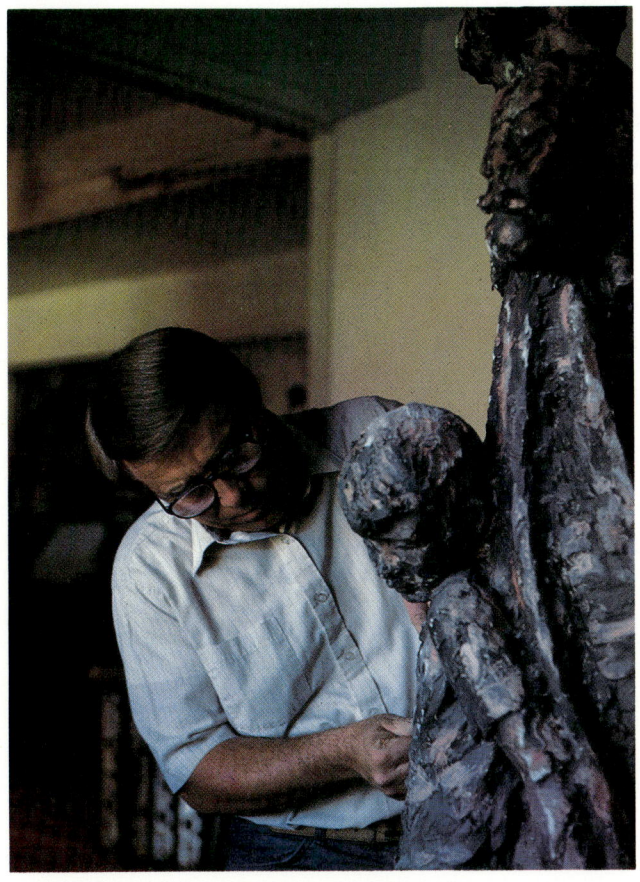

Dennis Smith. Fountain figure in bronze.

Instructions for Creating Art

1. Add as many kinds of artists as you can to the list given in the lesson. Do you know what is created by each kind of artist?

2. Now, look through magazines and other picture sources for examples of things artists produce. Try to find examples for some of the more unusual areas of art. Neatly cut out your pictures.

3. You may wish to arrange your pictures according to the senses, putting examples of things you smell in one area, things you can touch in another, things you can hear in another, and so on. Can you name the five senses? Try to find examples representing each sense. Make a pleasing **composition** of lines and shapes as you arrange your pictures.

4. Now, begin applying glue to each piece and placing it on your paper. Overlap the edges of your pictures as you place them, so that the entire surface of your paper is covered. Display your finished collage with others from your class.

Art Materials	
Construction paper	Magazines and other picture sources
Scissors	

Learning Outcomes

1. What is a *collage*?

2. How many different kinds of work produced by artists did you include in your collage?

3. What is the most unusual art area you added to your collage? What area would you most like to work in?

8 Drawing: Adding to an Object

Observing and Thinking Creatively

What objects do you visualize, or picture, when you think of a baseball? Maybe you associate a baseball with a catcher's mitt, a bat, a uniform, a trophy, a scoreboard, or a broken window. We often associate certain things with particular objects.

In this lesson, you will draw a picture of an object you see. Then, using your memory, you will add other things to your picture that you associate with the first, observed object. Look at the student art on these pages and see if you can identify the object the students drew from observation. Now, test your own memory and imagination as you add to the object your teacher provides. Use your knowledge of **shading**, **texture**, **mass**, and **composition** in your drawing.

Instructions for Creating Art

1. Choose the object you wish to draw. Study it from all sides. What kind of object is it? What other kinds of objects could you draw to go with it? How big will you make the object in relation to the things you will add from your memory? Where will you place it on your paper?

2. When you have decided what you are going to add to your picture, and how large your objects will be, begin drawing your picture.

3. Notice which areas of the object are light, and **shade** the dark areas. Decide how you will show the **texture**, the rough or smooth surface of your object. Try to make your drawing look as real as the actual object.

4. Now complete your drawing by adding other items that relate to the original object. In order to make something look real in a drawing, you must know exactly what it looks like. Looking at objects carefully, and then remembering, will help you improve your art.

Art Materials

Miscellaneous materials, such as bucket, bone, clock, hat, etc.

Paper

Pencil and eraser

Learning Outcomes

1. Explain why you chose the objects you added to your picture.

2. Describe how you showed textures in your drawing.

3. Tell which part of your picture looks most realistic, and explain why you think so.

9 An Animal Sketch

Observing and Thinking Creatively

Do you know where the earliest sketches of animals are found? Pictures of animals drawn by prehistoric people have been found on cave walls and cliffs. These animals can be recognized even though some of them, like the mammoth, are extinct today. What makes the animals recognizable is the simplicity and **accuracy** of their drawn **shapes**.

The chalk and oil pastel drawings by Peter Paul Rubens and Paul Thiebaud are also easily recognizable. Notice how each artist captured the main shape of the animal. The rabbit's body can be seen as different sized and shaped **ovals**. When the rabbit is sitting, the ovals bunch up. How many different ovals can you identify? What shapes make up the overall shape of the lion? What shapes make up the details?

After drawing the shape of the rabbit, Thiebaud made it look furry by **highlighting** and using **gradations** of **shading**. Notice how soft the rabbit's fur appears. How did Rubens make the lion's mane look wavy, full, and thick?

In this lesson, you will observe, study, and draw an animal of your choice using chalk or oil pastels. You will increase your awareness of shape and **proportion**, the relationship in size of one thing or part to another. You will also experiment with shading and line to show texture in your drawing.

Sir Peter Paul Rubens, Flemish, 1577–1640, Lion, c. 1614, Black and yellow chalk heightened with white, 9 15/16" × 11 1/8". National Gallery of Art, Washington. Ailsa Mellon Bruce Fund.

Wayne Thiebaud, Rabbit, 1966, pastel on paper, 14 3/4" × 19 1/2". Courtesy of Edwin A. Bergman.

Instructions for Creating Art

1. Choose an animal you would like to draw. You might draw a pet, an exotic animal, or an animal in a photograph. Perhaps you could visit a zoo or natural history museum. Observe and study your animal closely. Notice especially the animal's form and the texture of its hide, fur, feathers, or scales.

2. Practice making the shapes you see in your animal. Draw ovals, rectangles, squares, circles, triangles, and anything else you see. Then practice filling in the shapes with different **values** to show **form**. Smudge and blend lines and areas to create texture and gradation.

3. Next, put the shapes together in a sketch. Draw the main shapes first in light-colored chalk or oil pastel. Then add those that go inside and outside the main shapes. Show **contrast** and **depth** by using dark and light colors.

Art Materials	
Paper	Fixative (optional)
Colored chalk or oil pastels	Newspaper (to cover work area)

Learning Outcomes

1. Name three examples of basic shapes in your drawing.

2. Describe parts of your drawing where you created the look of fur, scales, feathers, or skin through lines and shading.

3. Tell which of the drawings by Rubens and Thiebaud you think is most skillfully drawn or shows the most feeling, and why.

10 Painting with Earth Colors

Observing and Thinking Creatively

When you decide to paint a picture, your teacher probably gives you paints to use, or perhaps your parents buy a box of watercolors for you. Today, all kinds of paints come ready-mixed, but long ago, people had to make their own.

Look at these pictures of animals painted on cave walls thousands of years ago. More than two hundred caves have been found decorated with animal paintings. Of them all, the wall paintings of houses, oxen, and red deer at Lascaux (la-skō) in France and Altamira (al-tə-mir-ə) in Spain are among the most beautiful and best preserved.

As you look at the photographs of these animals painted so long ago, what colors do you see? How do you think these early people got their paints?

Primitive people made paint by grinding colored iron ore into powder. They mixed the reddish ore, green hues of copper, and other brown, yellow, and reddish earth with plant juices, animal blood, soot, or fat to make them into paint. Can you see why these colors are called **earth colors**?

Most prehistoric cave paintings are of large animals, such as horses, mammoths, and bison. Sometimes humans appeared in these paintings in the form of stick figures.

We can only guess why people began to paint these pictures, but it seems likely that they were painted to tell about or bring about success in hunting.

In this lesson, you will paint a picture of a typical scene, using earth colors.

Instructions for Creating Art

1. Make a few practice sketches of common scenes from your life. What do you do in a typical day? You may want to illustrate yourself doing something that makes you feel good about yourself. You will use these sketches to plan your painting.

2. Rub a pale, dull color of chalk all over your paper. Use the side of the chalk, and rub it into the paper with a wad of soft tissue. Some of the chalk will come off, but most of it will be rubbed into the paper and will be the background for your painting.

3. Mix earth colors to paint your picture. You will need brown and black, and you will mix some brown into the red and the yellow to make dull earth colors.

4. Paint your scene with simple line drawings using earth colors. If someone found your drawing on a cliff or cave wall, what could he or she learn about you and your life?

Art Materials	
White paper	Container of water
Pencil and eraser	
Colored chalk	Mixing tray
Tempera paints	Newspaper (to cover work area)
Brushes	

Learning Outcomes

1. Describe earth colors and explain how they were made by ancient people.

2. Tell what colors you mixed to make different earth colors for your picture.

3. Tell the story message about life today that you showed in your picture.

21

11 Tints, Shades, and Tones

Observing and Thinking Creatively

What do you notice that is similar about the pictures shown here? Here is a clue: Can you find a place where white has been mixed with a color? Can you find a place where the artist has mixed black with a color? Or where gray has been mixed with colors? The artists all changed or varied their colors by adding white to make a **tint**, black to make a **shade**, and gray to make a **tone**. Artists lighten, darken, and **subdue** colors in this way.

In other ways, these pictures seem to be very different from each other. One is **representational**, with objects and people you can recognize. The other is more **abstract**. It has been changed so that it looks very little like the real world. Notice the different styles and ideas expressed by these artists.

Even when artists have different **styles** and use a variety of materials and techniques, they have a similar understanding of the effects of color and make decisions on ways to use it in their work.

In this lesson, you will mix tints, shades, and tones and use them in a design or picture.

Pablo Picasso, Spanish, 1881–1973. Family of Saltimbanques, *1905. Canvas, 83 3/4" × 90 3/8". National Gallery of Art, Washington, Chester Dale Collection.*

Robert Delaunay, French, 1885–1941, Political Drama, 1914, Collage, 35" × 26". National Gallery of Art, Washington. Gift of the Joseph H. Hazen Foundation, Inc.

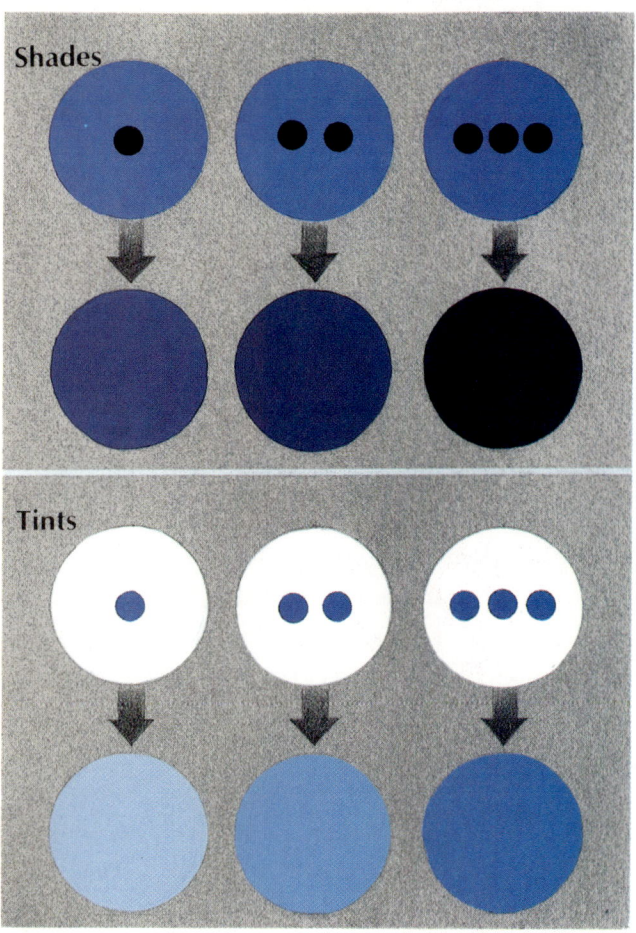

Instructions for Creating Art

1. Decide on the kind of picture you want to paint. You might paint a scene showing mood, an arrangement of objects, a picture with human or animal figures, or perhaps a bold, original design. Your picture may be abstract or representational. When you have an idea, lightly sketch it.

2. Select a few colors. Make shades by adding a small amount of black to each color. Tints are made by mixing white with color. For this lesson, you should begin with white and add a small amount of color to the white.

3. Now mix gray by adding a small amount of black to a lot of white. Make tones by adding gray to each color.

4. Use your shades, tints, and tones to paint your picture or design.

Art Materials	
Paper	Mixing tray
Tempera or other paints	Container of water
Brushes	Newspaper (to cover work area)

Learning Outcomes

1. Describe three ways that color can be changed.

2. Tell which colors you used and how many different shades, tints and tones you created for your picture.

3. Identify all the shapes and colors in the artworks shown here.

12 Imagining a Fantasy Tree

Observing and Thinking Creatively

How many different kinds of trees can you name? You may be familiar with fruit trees, pine trees, weeping willows, or sequoias. Like people, no two trees are alike. Each has its own unique shape, line, and style.

One way of creating **abstract** art is to take a familiar form and change it by adding unusual details, colors, or patterns. Jesse Allen is a modern American artist who uses these techniques in his paintings. He often combines animal forms that he observed while living in Kenya, Africa, painting them in jungle-like **landscapes**. Notice the unusual details in *The Banyon Tree*. What lines and shapes did he repeat in this painting?

The Tree of Light has a completely different mood than *The Banyon Tree*. Its use of pure, strong line and color are typical of the simplicity of Shaker design. Notice the **symmetry** of the tree. This design is perfectly balanced because parts on both sides of the center of the tree are the same.

What are the basic shapes used in the trees shown in this lesson? The overall shape of the tree, its leaves, and the pattern they form on the tree, as well as the appearance of the trunk, all contribute to a certain **mood**. In this lesson, you will design and paint a tree created from your imagination.

Jesse Allen, The Banyon Tree: Midmorning, Watercolor. Courtesy of Vorpal Galleries: San Francisco and New York.

Hannah Cohoon, The Tree of Light or Blazing Tree, Photography by courtesy of Hancock Shaker Village, Pittsfield, MA.

Instructions for Creating Art

1. Decide the basic shape and size of your tree. What feeling do you want to communicate with this tree? When you have an idea for your tree, draw its basic shape.

2. Decide what details you will add to your tree. What shape will the leaves be? Which shapes can be repeated to show a pattern and **unity**? You may wish to show other creatures or plants near the tree, or simply draw the tree alone. Add the details to your drawing.

3. When the drawing is finished, choose the colors you want to use. Repeating certain colors will unify your painting, so the parts seem to belong together. You may wish to show texture by using a dark color next to a lighter color. As you choose your colors, think about the feeling you want your tree to show. Also, decide on the weather, season, and time of day you will portray in your scene. Bright, warm colors like red, yellow, and orange seem to communicate a cheerful, lively feeling. Cooler colors, such as blue, green, and violet, seem more serene and quiet. Paint your tree with the colors of your choice.

4. When your fantasy tree is painted, display it with others from your class. How are the trees different? What moods can you identify in the different fantasy trees?

Art Materials	
Drawing paper	Container of water
Pencil and eraser	Paper towels
Tempera paints	Newspaper (to cover work area)
Brush	

Learning Outcomes

1. Tell the meaning of *symmetry*.

2. Describe what you did to express the special mood of your fantasy tree.

3. Tell whether your design is a good example of symmetry. Explain why or why not.

13 Oriental Art Designs

Observing and Thinking Creatively

Oriental art, which includes art from Japan, China, Taiwan, and other Asian countries, is characterized by its use of pure line. The Chinese are famous for their **calligraphy**, or beautiful handwriting. Their art frequently represents plants, flowers, animals, and other natural forms. It is often painted on silk scrolls. Sometimes the art includes a poem done in calligraphy. This adds to both the meaning and the design of the art.

Both Chinese and Japanese paintings usually use the concept of **foreground**. The lower the picture is placed on the paper, the nearer the object or place appears to the viewer.

Hokusai, one of the most famous Japanese artists, is known for his intricate, well-balanced designs. His skill with line is shown in *Tuning the Samisen*. Notice that there are no shadows or reflections in the picture.

The sketch of a monk by Chinese artist Liang K'ai shows how expressive even the simplest lines can be.

In this lesson, you will paint a simple, everyday scene, or a scene showing natural forms, in the Oriental manner. You will concentrate on drawing your scene with simple, well-designed lines.

Tzu-Hsi, Peonies and Cat Meowing at Pug Dog. *Field Museum of Natural History, Chicago.*

Liang K'ai, Li Po Chanting a Poem. Tokyo National Museum, Tokyo, Japan.

Hokusai, Tuning the Samisen. Edo period, Ukiyoe school. Paper sheets, unmounted. 9¾" × 8¼". Freer Gallery of Art, Smithsonian Institution, Washington, D.C.

Instructions for Creating Art

1. First, practice making different kinds of brush strokes. Gently squeeze your brush into a point and lightly draw thin, delicate lines. Practice pressing down heavily to make wider lines. Next, try making curves and swirls with your brush.

2. Decide on the scene you want to paint. Will you draw children playing a game, or perhaps someone working? You may wish to create a moment in nature, or a design of flowers, leaves, or grass. For other ideas, look for examples of Oriental art in encyclopedias and art books.

3. Make a few practice sketches of your scene. Experiment with the placement of the objects you want to include in your picture. Put the parts you want closest to the viewer lower down on your paper. Do you want to paint your scene on a long, vertical or horizontal piece of paper, like the Chinese scrolls?

4. Now, looking at your sketch, draw your design again, with brush and paint. Do not sketch it first in pencil. Display your finished Oriental design.

Art Materials

Sketch paper	Container of water
Pencil and eraser	Paper towels
Paints	Newspaper (to cover work area)
Brush	

Learning Outcomes

1. Name two characteristics of Oriental design.

2. Describe the Oriental art characteristics of your painting.

3. Which of the artworks here shows the most skillful use of line? Explain why you think it is best.

14 Printing with Natural Objects

Observing and Thinking Creatively

Have you ever been fingerprinted? If so, you probably know that no two fingerprints are alike. There are billions of people on earth, but no two have exactly the same patterns of lines and curves on their fingertips. Your fingerprint is a unique identification tag.

There are many things in nature that make unusual, fascinating prints. In this lesson, you will print some natural objects, such as vegetables, plants, feathers, shells, bones, and pieces of wood. To make a **press print**, or **stamp print**, you will press an inked object onto paper to transfer a design. Your print's **composition**, including **balance**, **space** usage, **line** direction, **color**, and **texture**, will be an original and unique design unlike that of any of your classmates.

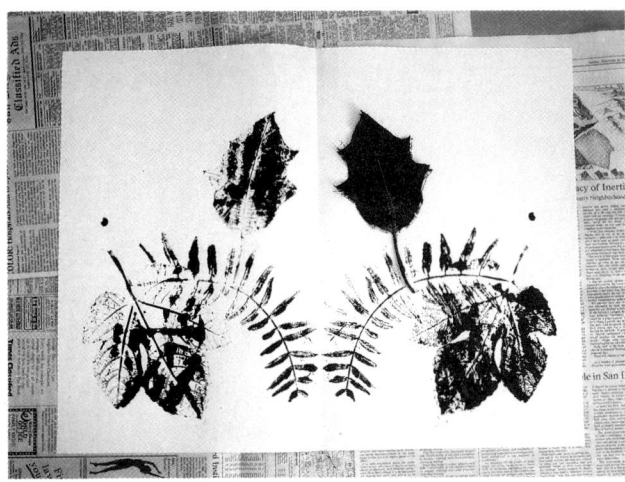

Instructions for Creating Art

1. Choose three or four natural objects on the basis of interesting shape, sturdiness, and uniqueness. Objects that are basically flat work best. You may want to use one type of object, such as three or four different kinds of leaves, or you may wish to use a mixed variety of objects.

2. Cover your work area with newspaper. Choose a color of ink or paint, and squeeze it onto a tray or a cookie sheet. Then roll it with a **brayer**, a rubber roller, until it is tacky, or sticky.

3. Lay your natural object on the inked surface and roll over it with the inked brayer so that both sides of the object are covered with ink. See the illustration above.

4. Carefully place the colored object inside a folded piece of paper. Rub the outside of the paper over every part of the object. Open the paper and carefully lift off the object. You will have two prints, one on each side of the fold.

5. Continue to ink and print objects in various positions, paying close attention to the overall composition of the print. Try overlapping and using several colors. Printing an object repeatedly without re-inking creates a three-dimensional effect.

6. To make your print unique, use a colored marker to draw in a small insect or other figure when your print is dry. Use a contrasting color, and outline it with a fine-tipped black pen for **emphasis**. What you draw will be the dominant feature, or **center of interest**, of your design.

Art Materials

Newspapers to cover work area	Soluble printing ink or tempera paint
18″ × 24″ blank newsprint	Tray or cookie sheet
Natural objects: vegetables, rocks, leaves, feathers, shells, bark, weeds, etc.	Colored markers
	Fine-tipped black pen
Brayer	Paper towels
Container of water	

Learning Outcomes

1. What is a *press print*?
2. Tell how you showed emphasis in your print design.
3. Describe parts of your print where texture is especially interesting.

15 Kinetic Art: Art That Moves

Observing and Thinking Creatively

Art often represents things that we recognize, such as people, animals, and landscapes. But some artists are interested mainly in lines, shapes, or colors. They want to create something unlike anything that has previously existed. Art without a recognizable object is called **non-objective** art.

Alexander Calder was one of the first artists to design shapes and hang them on wires. His hanging sculptures, or **mobiles**, were a kind of non-objective art called **kinetic sculpture**—sculpture that moves. Calder balanced shapes so that a slight breeze set the sculpture in motion. As the shapes are moved by air currents, they may appear to be lines and then **planes**, or flat surfaces, again. What other objects that move also have "mobile" in their name? For another example of a Calder mobile, turn to page 1.

George Rickey was also interested in creating kinetic sculpture. Look at the example of Rickey's sculpture in this lesson. How is it different from Calder's sculpture? Rickey's kinetic sculpture is not a mobile, but is called a **stabile**. It has a stationary or unmovable base and the other pieces move.

In this lesson, you will assemble a mobile. It may be realistic or it may be non-objective.

Alexander Calder, American, 1898–1976, Untitled, 1976, Aluminum and steel, 29' 10½" × 75'. National Gallery of Art, Washington. Gift of the Collectors Committee.

George Rickey, Three Red Lines, 1966. Lacquered stainless steel kinetic construction, 444" high. Hirshhorn Museum and Sculpture Garden, Smithsonian Institution.

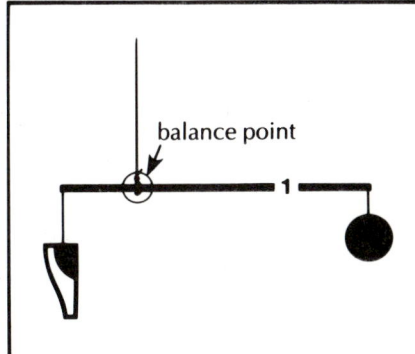

Attach two objects to mobile arm **1**. Loosely tie a string around the arm. Holding the arm by its string, move the string along the arm until you come to the point where the two objects balance. This is called the balance point.

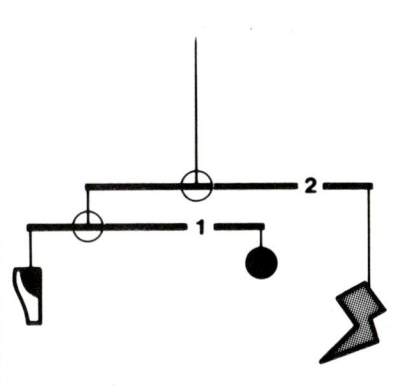

Mobile arm **1** is now a single piece that can be hung from mobile arm **2**. Tie a string around arm **2** and attach another object to balance against arm **1**. Move the string until arm **2** is balanced.

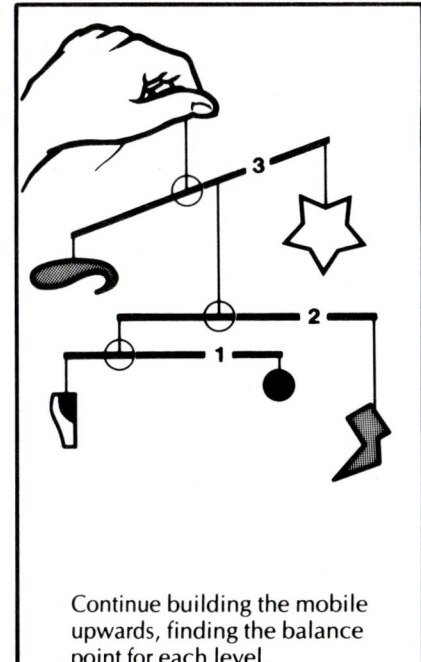

Continue building the mobile upwards, finding the balance point for each level.

Instructions for Creating Art

1. Decide on a theme for your mobile. You might choose to cut out shapes that represent your hobbies or a special interest. You might make a mobile for a book report, with the main characters represented in the mobile. Perhaps you would like to choose a theme of leaves, with many different leaf shapes making up your mobile. You may also wish to balance and experiment with a non-objective mobile of shapes.

2. Cut out your paper shapes. They may be flat, or you may choose to make parts that are three-dimensional and come out in different directions.

3. Follow the instructions shown in the illustration above.

4. Hang your finished mobile to display it.

Art Materials

White and colored stiff paper or thin cardboard

Scissors

Paste or glue

12″ and 16″ wire

Heavy black thread

Clear tape

Stapler

Assortment of objects: feathers, toothpicks, seeds, buttons, beans, etc.

Learning Outcomes

1. Name two forms of *kinetic art* and tell how they are alike and how they differ.

2. Tell whether your mobile shapes are *realistic* or *non-objective,* and explain how you decided what shapes to make.

3. Which of the examples of kinetic art shown here do you like better? Tell why you chose that example.

Exploring Art

Portraits and Biographies

In this unit, you have seen how artists express ideas and feelings in pictures, rather than words. For this activity, however, you will use both words and pictures to tell about someone you know. First, select someone willing to answer questions and pose for you. Then plan and write out questions that will reveal information about the person you chose.

Asking questions that can be answered "yes" or "no" will not give you the kind of information you need. Make up ten to fifteen questions similar to these: What do you like best about the people you live with? What do you like to do in your free time? What would you do if you had a million dollars?

When the person has answered all of your questions, organize the information into an interesting biographical paragraph. Leave a blank for the person's name so others can guess who it is.

Next, have the person pose for you. Study the person and look for interesting features. What makes this person look different from everyone else? Look at the portraits on this page. What can you tell about these people?

Draw your person's hair first. Then draw in the eyebrows, eyes, and eyelids. Eyes are about halfway down the head. Notice the shape and placement of the eyes. Do they turn up at the corners? Are they large, or small? Do they look close together, or are they spaced far apart?

Now draw in the nose, mouth, and chin. Add ears and neck if they show, with a collar or other details. On the back of a 12"×18" piece of paper in the person's favorite color, write his or her name. Mount the portrait and your biographical paragraph on the front, and display it. Can others in your class identify this person?

Pablo Picasso, Head of a Young Man, 1923. Conte crayon, 24½" × 18⅝", The Brooklyn Museum, Carll H. De Silver Fund.

Review

Using What You Have Learned

Le Haras du Pin, which means The Pin Horse Farm, was painted by French artist Raoul Dufy. He used many shapes and colors in this simple, sketchy watercolor painting. Apply the art ideas you studied in this unit as you examine *Le Haras du Pin.*

Raoul Dufy, Haras du Pin, 1932. Watercolor, 19¼" × 25". The Baltimore Museum of Art: Bequest of Sadie A. May, BMA 1951.295.

1. Identify and point out the basic **shapes** in this painting.

2. Can you find a place where a basic shape is repeated to form a **pattern** design? What shape is repeated?

3. Did Dufy use mainly **complementary** or **primary colors** in this picture? What makes you say so?

4. Where is the **center of interest** in this picture? What leads your eye to it?

5. Are the objects in this picture shown mostly with **contours,** or with **mass?** Why do you say so?

6. What is the **mood** or feeling expressed in this painting of a horse farm? Tell why you think so.

33

Unit 2

Exploring Art Elements

Henri Motte, The Trojan Horse, Corcoran Gallery, Washington, D.C.

The Roman poet Virgil wrote about a horse involved in the Trojan War, which took place about 1200 B.C. Greece and Troy had been at war. Then the Greeks placed a huge wooden horse outside the walls of Troy, and the Greek army sailed away. Hiding inside the horse, however, were several Greek warriors. The Trojans took the Greek horse into their city and celebrated their apparent victory over the Greeks. While the Trojans slept that night, the Greek warriors crept out of the horse and opened the city gates for the rest of their army, which had sailed back. The "Trojan horse" opened the way for a Greek victory over Troy.

The portrayal of the horse in art began with images drawn on the walls of prehistoric caves in Spain and France. Since that time, the beauty and grace of the horse have been **drawn**, **painted**, **carved**, and **engraved** by people in almost every culture.

The horse appears as **porcelain sculpture** in China, and is found on bronze monuments throughout Europe. These heavy war stallions are represented as huge and powerful, rather than the slender, fine-boned creatures found in Greek art.

Theodore Gericault, Horse Race at the Start, ca. 1820. Courtesy Giraudon/Art Resource.

Theodore Gericault drew and painted the horse almost exclusively because he thought the horse was the most beautiful animal in the world. Notice his skill in capturing the spirited feeling of the horses racing in the painting shown here.

In this unit, you will explore **line**, **shape**, **texture**, **form**, **color**, **value**, and **space**. You will become acquainted with the principles of **unity**, **balance**, **variety**, **emphasis**, and **rhythm**. As artists have done with horses throughout the ages, you will bring to life your unique ideas about what you see and what you imagine.

16 Complementary Color Changes

Observing and Thinking Creatively

Look at the color wheel in this lesson. Two colors directly across from one another on the color wheel are called **complementary colors**. When a color has some of its **complement**, or opposite color, added to it, the color changes and is not as bright. The color has changed in its **intensity**. Artists change colors in this way to create an effect or a mood.

Look at Henri Rousseau's painting, *Equatorial Jungle*. Some of the green leaves have been **neutralized** with red, the complement of green, until they are almost gray. Can you see a shimmer of red in places? Rousseau also mixed blue and gray into some of the paint for the leaves. How many different greens can you see in this painting?

In this lesson, you will change the color green by adding different amounts of its complement, red.

Henri Rousseau, French, 1844–1910, The Equatorial Jungle, 1909, Canvas, 55¼" × 51", National Gallery of Art, Washington. Chester Dale Collection.

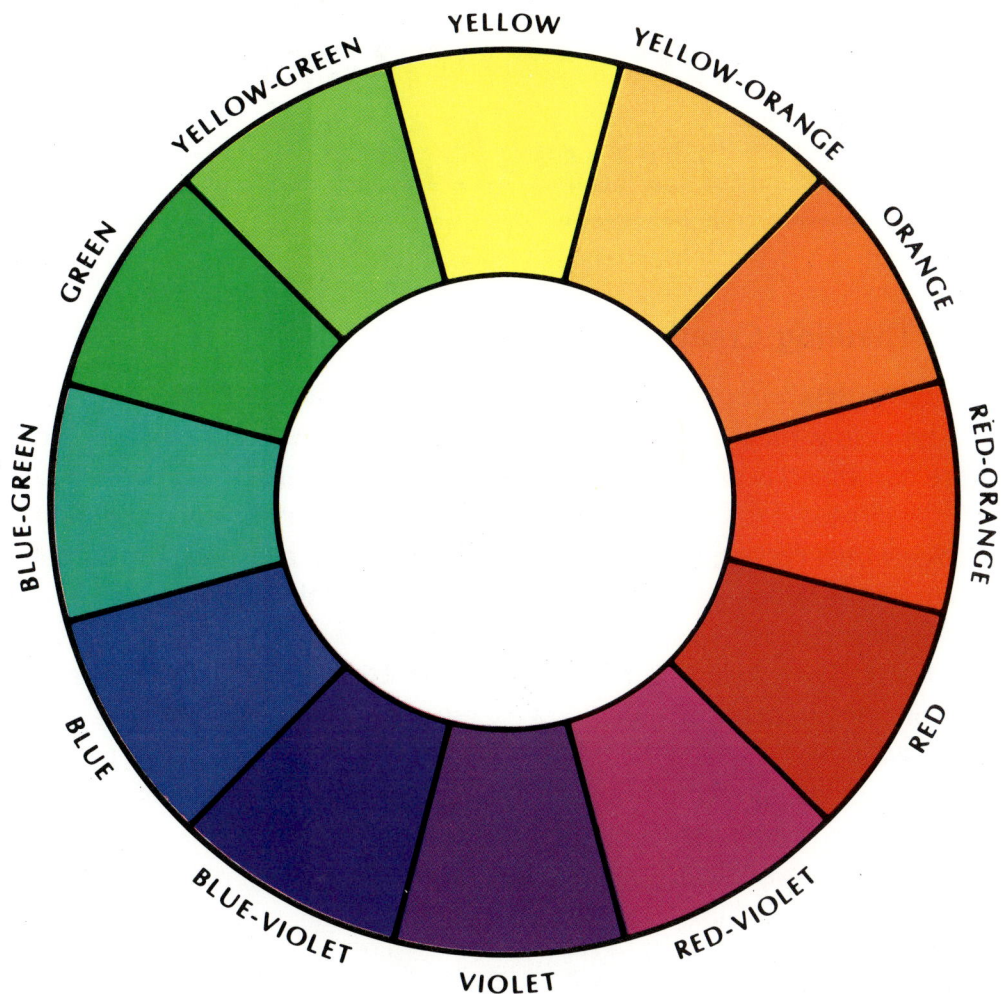

Instructions for Creating Art

1. Examine the colors of many leaves. Notice how many different greens exist in nature. Using tempera paint, mix many different variations of green by adding red and other colors.

2. Draw several leaves on a piece of paper. Have some of them overlap. Make several different shapes of leaves. You may wish to include some of the stem with some of your leaf designs.

3. Now, paint the leaves with your variety of green colors. If you want to, you may print a leaf by painting the back of it with a green tint and then pressing the painted side onto the paper.

Art Materials

- Variety of different colors and types of leaves
- Paper
- Tempera paints
- Mixing tray
- Brush
- Container of water
- Paper towels
- Newspaper (to cover work area)

Learning Outcomes

1. Describe what happens to a color when its *complement* is added to it.

2. Describe the greens you made and what you did to change them.

3. What is the mood of Rousseau's jungle scene? Does it seem friendly? Why do you think so?

17 Color Relationships

Observing and Thinking Creatively

Did you know that artists plan their color combinations? The colors they use and the way the colors are combined is called a **color scheme**.

Look at the color wheel on page 37. What is the lightest color on the wheel? What is the darkest? What are colors opposite one another on the color wheel called? Yellow and violet are examples of **complements**.

What are the colors next to violet? Red-violet and blue-violet are called **split complements** because they are split, or separated, by the true complement of yellow.

Examine Gauguin's painting of *Woman with Mango*. The artist has used blue-violet as a **dominant** color. Can you find the complement of blue-violet on the color wheel? Gauguin included this color, yellow, as part of his color scheme.

Complements can be split one step further to become a **triad**, three colors equally spaced on the color wheel. Umberto Boccioni uses the yellow-blue-red triad in his powerful painting *The City Rises*. Notice how he painted small brushstrokes of the three colors next to one another. His use of bold primary colors as this color scheme strengthens the impact of this painting.

In this lesson, you will create a painting using a color scheme of split complements or a triad of colors.

Paul Gauguin, Woman with Mango, 1892. Oil on canvas, 28⅝" × 17½". The Baltimore Museum of Art: The Cone Collection, formed by Dr. Claribel Cone and Miss Etta Cone of Baltimore, Maryland. BMA 1950.213.

Umberto Boccioni, The City Rises, 1910. Oil on canvas, 6'6½" × 9'10½". Collection, The Museum of Modern Art, New York, Mrs. Simon Guggenheim.

Instructions for Creating Art

1. Make several sketches of ideas for your painting. You may make a simple portrait of a person, as Gauguin did, or you may prefer to paint a landscape or nature scene. You might paint a still-life arrangement, or an abstract design. When you have a sketch you like, proceed to step 2.

2. Plan your colors by first looking at the color wheel in your book and choosing the dominant color. Now pick the split complement or the triad to that color.

3. Use the color scheme you have planned to make your painting. You may use other colors, too, but only in small amounts. The split complements or triad of colors should be the dominant colors in your painting or design.

Art Materials

Paper	Paper towels
Paints and brushes	Newspaper (to cover work area)
Mixing tray	
Container of water	Items for a still-life

Learning Outcomes

1. Give an example of *split complements* and *triad* color schemes.

2. Tell the color relationship of the colors you selected for your painting.

3. Which of the paintings shown here do you think uses color most effectively? What are the reasons for your choice?

18 Impressionism: Dots and Dabs of Color

Observing and Thinking Creatively

Look at the painting *Monet Painting in His Garden at Argentueil* by French artist Auguste Renoir. How did Renoir show the time of day in this picture? How is the light in the scene different from the light of noon? Because artists who painted in this style tried to catch *impressions,* an art critic named the style **Impressionism** in 1871.

The Impressionists were most interested in light and color, and painted mainly outdoors. They painted quickly to capture atmosphere and **mood** at different times of the day.

As you look at Renoir's picture of his friend Monet painting in the garden, notice the small strokes of color. Impressionists placed short brush strokes or dabs of pure color next to one another. When viewed from a distance, the colors seem to bounce off each other and mix, creating many other colors. This process is called **optical mixing.**

Georges Seurat used the Impressionist idea of mixing colors in a scientific, almost mathematical way. Instead of using short strokes of color, he applied thousands of tiny dots. Seurat was called a **Pointillist.** Look closely at the study he did for *Sunday Afternoon on the Island of La Grande Jatte.* How many examples of **complementary colors** placed together can you find?

The Impressionists avoided using black because it is seldom seen in nature. What colors were used to make up the shadows in these paintings?

In this lesson, you will paint a scene by using dots, dabs, or separate brushstrokes of pure color.

Pierre Auguste Renoir, Monet Painting in His Garden at Argentueil, *1873, Wadsworth Atheneum, Hartford, Connecticut.*

Georges Seurat, Study for "La Grande Jatte", 1884/1885, Wood, 6¼" × 9⅞", National Gallery of Art, Washington, Ailsa Mellon Bruce Collection.

Instructions for Creating Art

1. Lightly sketch an outdoor scene that includes trees and plants. If you want to, add people to your scene. Decide what time of day you will show in your scene. How much light is there at that time? The more light there is, the brighter the colors should be.

2. You may use a brush or a cotton swab to dab on dots and strokes of color. Use only the colors of the rainbow. Put different colors, such as yellow and blue, next to one another. When viewed from a distance, they will look green.

3. Use many brushstrokes of several colors to make your picture. Include colors that will make your painting look as if it is a bright, sunny day outdoors.

4. Give your painting a title and display it.

Art Materials

Paper	Container of water
Pencil and eraser	Paper towels
Mixing tray	Newspaper (to cover work area)
Tempera paint	
Cotton swabs	

Learning Outcomes

1. Name two characteristics of the *Impressionist* style of painting.

2. What colors did you place next to one another in your painting? What colors resulted from *optical mixing?*

3. Do you prefer the exactness of Seurat's Pointillism, or the freer style of Renoir? Explain the reasons for your choice.

19 Painting to Music

Observing and Thinking Creatively

What **color** do you associate with excitement? If you wanted to express the idea of loneliness or sadness, what shapes and patterns would you choose? Expressing feelings and mood in art is a kind of **abstract** art. It can help us increase our ability to understand and communicate ideas and emotions.

One style of abstract art can be created by listening to music and then painting the mood of the music. Colors, shapes, textures, pattern, rhythm, space, and line all contribute to the **mood** of an artwork. If you wanted to express a warm, happy mood, you might choose to cover your paper with yellow and orange shapes arranged so that they were touching each other. A single tiny splotch of blue against a blank white background might communicate loneliness.

Look at the student artworks in this lesson, and guess what kind of music was playing when each of them was painted.

In this lesson, you will use a process of **association** to create four different artworks. You will listen to four different kinds of music, and then paint the colors, rhythms, and shapes that your imagination associates or links with each musical piece.

Instructions for Creating Art

1. With your teacher and classmates, select four different kinds of music. You might consider listening to a ballad, rock music, music with a fast tempo, and music with a slow tempo. Whatever you choose should not have lyrics, because words would suggest images to you.

2. Divide an 18" × 24" piece of art paper into four equal squares, or use four separate, smaller sheets of paper. Place tape on both the horizontal and vertical dividing lines to prevent your paintings from running into each other.

3. Close your eyes and listen to one of the music selections, letting colors and images flash through your mind. Then begin to paint, keeping in tempo with the music whether it is fast or slow, smooth or rhythmic. Paint rhythm and sound, not pictures of realistic objects. Try to create a texture that fits the music. Is it smooth, rough, or bumpy? What shapes and lines do you imagine for this music? Repeat this process with the other musical selections.

4. Write the title of each piece of music on the back of each artwork, along with the title of your painting. Display them with others in your class. Are any of the paintings similar?

Art Materials

18" × 24" or small sheets of paper	Mixing tray
Cellophane tape	Fine felt-tip markers
Watercolors or tempera paints	Container of water
Various sizes and shapes of brushes	Newspaper (to cover work area)

Learning Outcomes

1. What does *association* mean?

2. Describe how you showed the rhythm, beat, or mood of the music in your artworks.

3. Choose your best work and tell how it expresses a piece of music.

20 Watercolor Techniques

Observing and Thinking Creatively

Have you noticed how the colors in a sunset seem to spill over into one another, mixing and merging together? The same thing happens in a rainbow, a reflection in a lake, and in the delicate colors of blossoms. **Watercolor** paints blend well, are **transparent**, allowing light to pass through them, and produce a soft effect. They are particularly well-suited to painting these kinds of scenes. Unlike oil or acrylic paints, watercolors are used to achieve a looser, freer, less detailed method of painting.

Many interesting effects can be achieved with watercolors. Examine the watercolor of a red canna lily by Georgia O'Keeffe on this page. Observe how the artist has achieved a depth of color while maintaining a softness of lines and details. O'Keeffe is known for painting images from nature with precision and clarity. Notice the way John Singer Sargent used color to create texture in his painting, *Muddy Alligators*.

In this lesson, you will experiment with and practice a variety of watercolor techniques to create different kinds of lines, textures, and mood. Then you will use your favorite techniques to paint one or more flowers.

Georgia O'Keeffe, Red Canna, 1920, watercolor. Yale University Art Gallery, Gift of George Hopper Fitch, BA 1932, and Mrs. Fitch.

John Singer Sargent, 1856-1925, American, 20th century, Muddy Alligators, Water color on paper, 13⅝" × 20⅞", Worcester Art Museum.

Instructions for Creating Art

1. Using round and flat brushes of varying widths and sizes, experiment with several kinds of strokes. A quick tapered stroke is made by pressing the brush down on the paper, then lifting and turning it slightly. Alternate thick and thin wavy lines by varying pressure on the brush. Be sure to rinse out your brush when you change colors.

2. Make a **wash**—a transparent, even sweep of color. A **gradated wash** has more pigment, or color, at the bottom, creating a gradated effect of light at the top which gradually becomes dark.

3. With a flat brush, stroke one color across the page. Then, when the first color has dried, stroke on another color that overlaps the first. The two hues will blend together and make a third color.

4. To achieve texture, dip a brush in paint and then remove most of the moisture by pressing it between paper towels. Brushstrokes made with this almost dry brush will leave a strip of broken color.

5. Use a sponge dipped in paint to add color. Use a clean, damp sponge or brush to lift off or lighten color.

6. Dip an old, dry toothbrush in thick watercolor. Rub your thumb across the bristles to splatter paint on your paper.

7. Now, paint a picture of a flower. Use a pencil to very lightly sketch the contours and details of a single flower or a simple arrangement of flowers. Then add color and details.

Art Materials

18" × 24" white construction paper	Round and flat brushes
Pencil and eraser	Small sponge, old toothbrush
Watercolor paper	Paper towels
Watercolor paints	Newspaper (to cover work area)
Container of water	

Learning Outcomes

1. Name two characteristics of watercolors.

2. Describe the techniques you used to paint your flower.

3. Tell which watercolor technique you like most and which you like least, and why.

21 A Watercolor Waterscape

Observing and Thinking Creatively

Watercolor paints are one of the most effective mediums for painting **waterscapes**—scenes with water. Different effects are created depending on the degree of dampness of the paper. The wetter the paper is, the more the colors will spread, creating a soft, hazy look. Other effects are achieved by allowing one color to dry before adding another to it.

Winslow Homer's painting of the *Mink Pond* shows a dark pool with muddy greens above and browns below. He reveals a swimming bass that can be seen above and below the water line, a poised frog, and the white water lily. Can you tell what has captured the attention of the fish and the frog?

Notice the **composition** of color in Homer's *Mink Pond*. Where are the **primary colors** placed? Where are the violets and greens? Which **reflections** can you see?

Reflections on water can double the beauty and interest of a particular scene. They can also create **symmetry** by repeating shapes. Notice the reflections in this pond scene. How are the colors Homer used in the reflection different from the colors of the object itself? Reflections often are made of **tones** of original colors. Do you remember how tones are made from Lesson 11?

Now look at the waterscape by artist John Marin. How does his style differ from Homer's? How did Marin create the illusion of movement in the water?

In this lesson, you will paint a waterscape with reflections. It may be in a realistic style similar to Winslow Homer's, or it may be painted with looser, freer brushstrokes like the work of John Marin.

Winslow Homer, Mink Pond, 1891. Drawing, watercolor over graphite on heavy white wove paper, 13¾" × 19⅘". Courtesy of the Fogg Art Museum, Harvard University. Bequest of Grenville L. Winthrop.

John Marin, Cape, Split, and Boat, *San Diego Museum of Art.*

Instructions for Creating Art

1. Experiment with achieving different effects of water by dampening your paper in different degrees and then painting on it. Let some paint dry and paint over it. Add a brush of water to paint that has already dried. Try a variety of experiments. Mix green and blue in different amounts.

2. When you have achieved a style of making water that you like, decide what kind of picture you want to paint. You may paint a waterscape of a stream, pond, waterfall, ocean, lake, bay, or puddle. What objects will you add to your scene? You might add animals, fish, boats, plants, and so on. Are there ripples or waves? Will you show movement or rhythm in your water?

3. Make practice sketches of your idea. You may wish to add reflections to your picture. To do that, you must decide where the sun is, and which direction the reflections would face. Be sure your reflections show the opposite, mirror-view of the objects being reflected.

4. Now, very lightly sketch your scene on your paper and begin to paint it. If you have included reflections, decide what colors they will be, and mix those colors. When your painting is finished, display it.

Art Materials	
Sketch paper	Brush
Drawing paper	Paper towels
Watercolors	Newspaper (to cover work area)
Mixing tray	

Learning Outcomes

1. Tell how dampness of paper affects watercolor.

2. Describe your method of painting water in your picture. If you included reflections, describe the colors you used to paint them.

3. Which of the waterscapes by Homer and Marin do you prefer? Give the reasons for your choice.

22 Above the Blue Horizon

Observing and Thinking Creatively

Whenever an artist includes earth and sky in a painting, he or she must decide where the **horizon** will be. The horizon is an actual or imaginary line where the earth and sky seem to meet. "Horizon" is the root for **horizontal**.

Observe Peter Hurd's painting, *Eve of St. John*. Can you find the horizon line? It is placed in the very center of the picture. The girl is in the **foreground**, the part of the painting that appears to be in the front, closest to the viewer. **Middle ground** refers to the parts of a picture that are in the middle. What objects are in the middle ground of this painting? The parts of a picture that are in the distance, behind those in the foreground and middle ground, are said to be located in the **background**. What makes up the background of this painting?

Can you guess what time of day it is from the sky? Notice how yellow gradually blends with blue to create a soft green in the middle area of the sky.

Now look at *View of Toledo*, by El Greco, a Greek artist who became famous in Spain during the sixteenth century. This is not an accurate view—it does not really represent the way the city of Toledo looked. El Greco rearranged the city's **topography**, or physical features, to make it appear more dramatic. Can you identify the parts of the painting that are in the foreground, middle ground, and background? Notice the colors El Greco mixed to paint clouds. How does the sky contribute to the **mood** of the painting? Where is the horizon line?

In this lesson, you will paint a scene with a horizon line, a foreground, a middle ground, and a background. The sky you paint will contribute to the mood of your picture.

Peter Hurd, Eve of St. John, *San Diego Museum of Art Collection.*

El Greco, View of Toledo, *Oil on canvas, 47¾ × 42¾ inches, The Metropolitan Museum of Art, Bequest of Mrs. H. O. Havemeyer, 1929, The H. O. Havemeyer Collection, 29.100.6.*

Instructions for Creating Art

1. Think of an outdoor scene you would like to paint. Decide what objects you will place in the foreground, middle ground, and background of your scene. Decide what time of day and what kind of weather you will represent in the sky you paint. Sunny weather and midday will look bright and will require light colors. Stormy weather, early morning, and evening are shown with darker hues.

2. Make some practice sketches of your scene, experimenting with placement of objects. Where will your horizon line be?

3. Dampen your paper before you begin. First, paint in the sky and clouds of your picture. Blend colors to show time of day and mood. Then add trees, hills, and other faraway things in the background. Blend the edges a little and keep the colors faint and hazy to give the idea of distance. Let the background dry before painting the next part.

4. Next, paint in the objects in the middle ground of your picture. These things are a little closer and have more detail, but they should still have a soft, fuzzy look.

5. When the middle ground is almost completely dry, paint in the things that are closest to you. Paint leaves, rocks, and small plants with sharp, clear details to show how close they are. Add color with a brush that is almost dry.

6. Display your finished landscape.

Art Materials

Sketch paper	Container of water
Drawing paper	Paper towels
Watercolor or tempera paints	Newspaper (to cover work area)
Mixing tray	
Brushes	

Learning Outcomes

1. Explain the meaning of *horizon*.

2. Describe how you showed time of day and mood with the sky you painted.

3. What is the most successful part of your painting? Why do you think so?

23 Art Styles of the Renaissance

Observing and Thinking Creatively

The term **Renaissance** refers to the rebirth of arts that took place in Europe during the fourteenth through the seventeenth centuries. Artists turned to the classical balance of Greek and Roman art. Plant, animal, and human forms took on a new look of **realism** as they were recreated with great detail and accuracy.

Italy was the center of this rebirth of art and the home of two of the greatest artists in history, Leonardo da Vinci and Michelangelo Buonarroti. Look at da Vinci's portrait of *Mona Lisa*. What kind of mood do you think she was in when he painted this expression? Da Vinci captured her sense of quiet amusement. Notice the skill displayed in the modeling of her lips. The skin of Mona Lisa's face seems to have a hidden radiance, or glow. Da Vinci was able to make light and shade merge unnoticeably in this portrait.

Michelangelo was a painter, a sculptor, and an architect. He painted a picture that covers the entire ceiling of the Sistine Chapel in Rome, and he was a master of creating human form. Observe the perfect **balance** and **proportions** in his figures of Mary and the dead Christ in the *Pieta*. This work was carved from a single block of marble.

A third genius of the Renaissance was German engraver Albrecht Dürer. His paintings and prints are full of carefully drawn details. What details make the sketch shown here look so realistic?

In this lesson, you will increase your sense of accuracy by drawing a very detailed, realistic picture of a person or object.

Leonardo da Vinci, Mona Lisa, 1503–1506. Oil on panel, 30" × 21". The Louvre, Paris.

Michelangelo Buonarroti, Pieta, St. Peter's Basilica, Rome, Italy. Vatican Museums and Galleries, Vatican City, Rome, Italy. Courtesy SCALA/Art Resource.

Albrecht Dürer, Young Woman in Netherlandish Dress, 1521. Brush and brown and white ink on gray-violet prepared paper, 11 1/8" × 7 3/4". National Gallery of Art, Washington. Widener Collection.

Instructions for Creating Art

1. Choose a person or object to draw. You may look at pictures of your subject, or draw the actual person or object. Make sketches of your subject until you have one you like.

2. Now look closely at the subject you chose. Notice the different values or shades, and the placement of details. After you have drawn the basic contours or shapes of your object, begin to add details. Keep in mind the proportions of the details, as well as their basic shapes.

3. When you have completed your drawing, color it with the medium of your choice and display it.

Art Materials

Drawing paper

Pencil and eraser

Paints and brushes

Container of water

Paper towels

Newspaper (to cover work area)

Learning Outcomes

1. Name two features of the *Mona Lisa* which make it a great artwork.

2. Explain how your artwork is similar to the Renaissance art in this lesson.

3. Which artwork shown here best shows human form? Why do you think it is better than the others?

24 Designing Round Art

Observing and Thinking Creatively

Look around and see how many round shapes you can identify. Coins, clocks, and pencil erasers are circular **shapes** familiar to us. The circle has been used in many ways in art. Can you think of artistic circles different from those shown here?

The stained-glass window was designed by Henri Matisse for a church, and was made from a model of paper cutouts. His design is perfectly balanced. When a circle has a center point with lines extending from it, it has **radial balance**. A wheel is a good example of radial balance. Which picture in this lesson shows radial design produced on a computer?

Things in nature and art that have radial balance are very **symmetrical**. When the parts radiating from the center are repeated over and over, pattern is formed. Which parts of the stained-glass window design are repeated? Frank Stella's design uses **asymmetrical** balance. The two sides of the artwork are not exactly alike, but still look balanced.

In this lesson, you will use radial balance to create pattern for a piece of round art.

Frank Stella, Sinjerli Variation 1, 1968. Private collection of Harry N. Abrams Family. Currently hanging in the lobby at One Seaport Plaza, New York, NY.

Henri Matisse, Abby Aldrich Rockefeller Memorial Window, Union Church of Pocantico Hills, Sleepy Hollow Restorations, Tarrytown, New York.

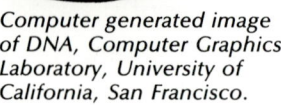

Computer generated image of DNA, Computer Graphics Laboratory, University of California, San Francisco.

Instructions for Creating Art

1. Using a compass, draw a very large circle on a piece of construction paper. Then cut out your circle and fold it in half. Fold it in half again, and then fold it one more time. Your paper will have a triangle shape.

2. Now, using a pencil, make a design on the exposed triangle of your paper. You may want to make several practice designs on a piece of scratch paper first. Use lines and shapes to make your design.

3. Next, color your design with crayons. Make all of your circles the same color, all of your squares the same color, and so on, so that your design will have unity.

4. When your design is colored, fold that section down on top of the blank section next to it. Using the rounded part of your scissors, press on the back side of the designed section. The design will transfer lightly to the new section.

5. Darken the lines and color in the new section just as you did the first one. Continue transferring the design until the entire circle has been colored.

6. When all the sections are filled in, you will have a unique example of round art with radial balance.

Art Materials

Construction paper

Pencil and eraser

Scissors

Crayons

Newspaper (to cover work area)

THINK SAFETY

Learning Outcomes

1. What is *radial balance*?

2. Describe how you showed pattern in your design.

3. Name your favorite example of radial art in the lesson. Why do you like it best?

25 Medal and Pendant Sculpture

Observing and Thinking Creatively

Long ago, kings and queens wore gold or silver **medallions**, or large **medals**, displayed around their necks on heavy chains. The medallions were symbols of their power and position, and usually contained special words or pictures related to the monarch's rule or ancestry. Observe the medal worn by King Henry VII in the painting by Hans Holbein II.

The idea of medallions has passed down through the ages. What modern examples can you name? Olympic winners are given medals made of gold, silver, or bronze that feature special **symbols** of the games. Military medals given to soldiers and officers represent rank, achievement, or heroism. Intricate carved, sculpted, cast, or embossed medallions may be worn as ornamental **pendants**, like the elephant pendant pictured in this lesson. Modern kings and queens still wear certain medals representing their position.

In this lesson, you will create an original medal, as a **relief** sculpture, or a pendant out of baker's clay. Relief refers to art in which figures or designs rise up from a flat background. You may design an award or symbol of achievement or excellence, or you may choose to make a piece of jewelry.

Hans Holbein, *Henry VIII*, Rome National Gallery.

Olympic Medal

Purple Heart Medal

Instructions for Creating Art

1. First, decide whether you are going to make a medal or a pendant. If it is to be a medal, what will it represent? You might choose to use a symbol in your design. Make several sketches until you have a design that you like. Add any details you want to include.

2. Cover your desk with newspaper and a sheet of wax paper sprinkled with flour to prevent your clay from sticking. Begin with an egg-sized ball of baker's clay. You may use oil-based or water-based clay instead, if you prefer. Do not use flour with these types of clay. Experiment with making different shapes.

3. Now begin forming your medal or pendant, following your sketched design as closely as possible. Details can be created by adding very small coils or balls of clay, or gouging out small bits of clay. Create texture by pressing a pencil, comb, coin, or other object into the clay.

4. When your medallion is finished, push and twist a straw through the top to create a hole for stringing.

5. If you used baker's clay, bake your medal or pendant in an oven at 350 degrees F. about an hour. You may fire water-based clay pieces in a **kiln**.

6. When your piece has cooled, paint it with tempera paints, let it dry, and shellac it. String your finished medallion with yarn, ribbon, or a chain.

Art Materials

Paper	Tempera paints and brushes
Pencil and eraser	Container of water
Baker's clay, oil-based, or water-based clay	Plastic straw
	Shellac
Wax paper and flour	Yarn, ribbon, or a chain
Cookie sheet (for baking medal)	Newspaper (to cover work area)

Learning Outcomes

1. Name three uses for medals.

2. Tell what colors you used for your piece, and why you chose them.

3. Tell what your medallion represents, and explain any symbols you used.

26 Painting Focus: Realism

Observing and Thinking Creatively

Much like photographs, the three paintings here show nature, people, and objects that the artists actually saw. This style of art is called realism. The realist artists often painted lively outdoor scenes, landscapes, portraits, and still life arrangements with great accuracy.

Thomas Eakins, one of the greatest American realists, painted natural scenes. His painting of a man in a scull, an oar-powered racing shell, shows Eakins' precise sense of proportion and detail.

Winslow Homer was first a printmaker, but is known for painting landscapes and the sea. He emphasized light and shadow in his work. Notice how the bright, sunny light in *Snap the Whip* adds to the happy mood of the painting. What realistic details did he portray in this scene?

Look closely at *My Gems* by William Harnett, a silver engraver who painted in the last quarter of the nineteenth century. Notice how precisely he rendered the objects in his still-life arrangement. And what an assortment of objects is on the table! Harnett thought of these objects as his gems. He chose them carefully because he wanted to show people what was important to him. Besides music, what else can you see that Harnett valued? Would any of these objects be your gems?

In this lesson, you will paint a still-life arrangement of your gems. You will discuss your painting with a classmate, increasing both your own and your classmate's awareness of the things you value. You will experiment with arrangement and details in painting your gems in a realistic way.

Thomas Eakins, Max Schmidt in a Single Scull, 1871. *Oil on canvas, 32¼" × 46¼". The Metropolitan Museum of Art, Alfred N. Punnett Fund and Gift of George D. Pratt, 1934. (34.92)*

Winslow Homer, Snap the Whip, The Butler Institute of American Art, Youngstown, Ohio

William M. Harnett, American, 1848–1892, My Gems, 1888. Wood, 18 × 14 inches. National Gallery of Art, Washington, Gift of the Avalon Foundation.

Instructions for Creating Art

1. Think about the things that have special meaning or value for you, your "gems." Gather them together, and arrange them on a flat surface. Be conscious of each object's position and experiment with the grouping. Consider the size of each object. What do you want to emphasize? What might be almost hidden? How will you balance the objects?

2. Try using the rule of compensation from lesson 5. The bigger the mass, the more the mass is toward the center. The smaller the mass, the more it is toward the edge. Observe how Harnett arranged the objects in his painting. What do you see first when you look at his picture?

3. Next, sketch your still-life composition. Then mix paint to match the colors of the items you chose. Paint your still-life arrangement of gems to look exactly as you see it.

4. Now choose a classmate and discuss each other's paintings. What do the objects tell about the values and interests of the artists?

Art Materials	
Personal objects	Mixing tray
Drawing paper	Container of water
Paints and brushes	Paper towels

Learning Outcomes

1. What is meant by **realism** in art?

2. Describe how you arranged your still life to reveal which objects are most important to you.

3. Tell which object in your painting appears the most real, and why.

27 Painting Animal Portraits

Observing and Thinking Creatively

Throughout history, artists have painted pictures of animals. Ancient European cave dwellers painted bison and deer to gain power over them in the hunt. Clans among North American Indian tribes honored their animal protectors, who came to them in visions or dreams, by representing them on totem poles. Other artists, like Englishman Edwin Landseer, painted portraits of favorite pets.

Landseer painted animals in a **realistic** style. The dogs shown here not only look like a hound and terrier, but they seem to have the qualities of dignity and impudence. Observe the details in their faces. Notice the lines and shading around the eyes which show the dogs' unique expressions and personalities. Which dog shows poise and nobility? Which may be a bit rude on occasion? Landseer has made it obvious.

The personality of an animal or human can best be seen in a portrait which shows the subject's face. In this lesson, you will paint an animal portrait. You will increase your awareness of details, and you will experiment with shape, form, color, **proportion** and brushstrokes to show the animal's personality.

Sir Edwin Landseer, Dignity and Impudence, *1839, Tate Gallery, London.*

Instructions for Creating Art

1. First, choose a favorite animal to paint. It may be your pet or an animal you especially like. Think about the personality of the animal. Perhaps it looks sad, or wise, or lively. Study pictures of the animal. If possible, sketch the actual animal.

2. Next, practice sketching your animal's face. Experiment with front and side views. You may wish to divide the head into the ear, eye, and nose areas. Identify the basic shapes and proportions. Notice where the eyes are in relation to the nose on each of Landseer's dogs. Observe how the ears are attached to the head. Practice drawing and placing the eyes and ears accurately on the face. Try to show personality through lines, color, and strokes, and practice some of Landseer's techniques. Complete your drawing.

3. Now paint your animal portrait. Concentrate on forms, lines, and strokes that reveal your animal's personality. Carefully mix your paints to create the exact color of the animal.

Art Materials

Pictures of animals	Mixing tray
Drawing paper	Container of water
Pencil and eraser	
Paints and brushes	Paper towels

Learning Outcomes

1. Name three ways animals have been used as subjects in art.

2. Describe how you expressed the personality of the animal you portrayed.

3. Describe the pose you selected for your animal portrait, and explain why you chose it.

28 From Realism to Abstraction

Observing and Thinking Creatively

Abstract art usually uses bright colors, sharp edges, geometric shapes, and interesting contrasts to create a mood. Sometimes abstract art simply shows an artist's emotional response to an object or idea. Details may be minimized, proportions **distorted**, and unusual color schemes used. **Nonobjective** art occurs when abstraction departs completely from realism.

Henri Matisse was a French artist who enjoyed changing the usual form of an object. His versions emphasized the pure idea of the object, and are a type of abstract art. To create the cutouts for the snail shown here, he first picked up a real snail and examined it closely. Then he drew it from every angle possible, noting its texture, color, and construction.

Observe the cut out paper shapes Matisse used in his snail of many colors. Can you see how the simple blue rectangle represents the foot of the snail? Notice which parts of a snail Matisse omitted, and which parts he thought were essential.

In this lesson, you will create an abstract cutout design of an object.

Henri Matisse, The Snail, 1952, Tate Gallery, London.

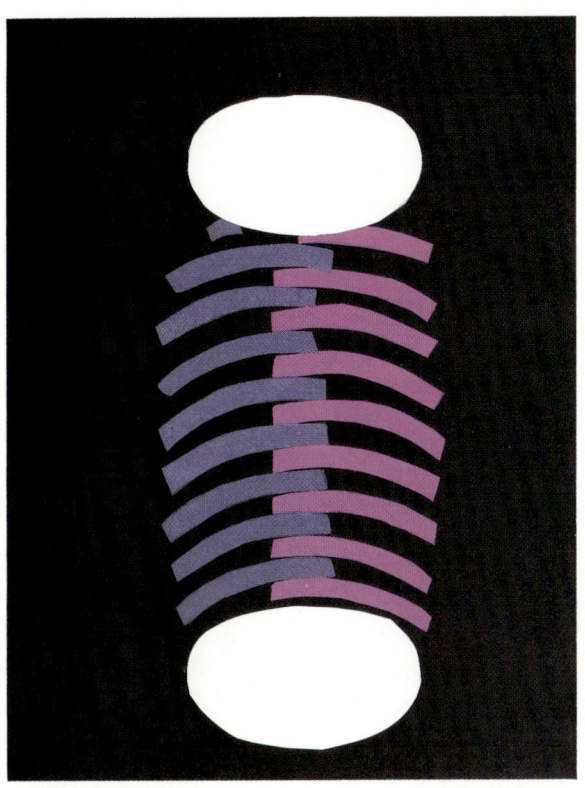

Instructions for Creating Art

1. Choose an object with an interesting shape and study it. Sketch it from several angles. Examine how it is built. Does it have a center? What basic shapes compose it? Observe the texture and colors of your object.

2. Now draw the general outer shape of your object. What idea does it give you? Next, draw only the inside parts of your object, without any outside lines. Think about what color reminds you of the feeling or idea of the object. Notice curved and straight lines, light and dark values, and small and large shapes.

3. When you find a shape that seems to capture the idea of your object, practice distorting or changing it to make a more pure, simple shape.

4. Choose one or more colors for your shape, and cut it out of colored paper. Mount the shapes on a sheet of a different color, and display your abstract cutout design. Can your classmates guess what the real object was?

Art Materials

A variety of objects such as a shell, spoon, corncob, flower, leaf, model, toy, piece of fruit, etc.

Sketch paper

Pencil and eraser

Colored construction paper

Scissors

Glue or paste

Learning Outcomes

1. Name two ways of making *abstract* art.

2. Describe how you distorted the shape you made of an object.

3. What parts of your object did you leave out of your cutout design? How did you decide which parts to keep and which parts to omit?

29 Two-View Portraits

Observing and Thinking Creatively

For thousands of years pictures were painted to show what a person or thing looked like. With the invention of the camera, however, artists became less concerned about showing **realistic** pictures. Artists began painting pictures that told a story or showed **mood** or personality. Sometimes artists are only concerned with expressing an idea, an emotion, or an impression.

Pablo Picasso, an artist who lived from 1881-1973, used many different painting styles during his life. He invented a **style** or way of expressing called **Cubism**, which was unlike any art that had ever been created. Picasso observed that figures and objects exist "in the round." The front, back, and side areas of a person exist all at once, even though they cannot be seen all at once from a single fixed position. He aimed to show all those parts at once on a flat surface, creating a **distorted** picture. In *Girl Before a Mirror*, Picasso shows both the **profile** and the front view of the girl's face.

In this lesson, you will create a portrait of a classmate in the Cubist style.

Pablo Picasso, Girl Before a Mirror, 1932. Oil on canvas, 64" × 51¼". Collection, The Museum of Modern Art, New York. Gift of Mrs. Simon Guggenheim.

Instructions for Creating Art

1. Using a classmate for a model, make several drawings showing the profile, and several other drawings showing the front view of the person's face and head.

2. On another sheet of paper, combine one drawing of a profile with a drawing of the front view. Draw the person's profile so that it fits into the full-face view.

3. When you are satisfied with your drawing, paint it. To emphasize the distortion of your picture, paint it with colors not usually seen for a person's face and hair. Cover the entire paper surface with paint.

4. If you wish to distort your picture even more, change the shapes of some of the parts of the face. You may also add lines, shapes, and patterns.

5. Display your finished portrait with others from your class. Can you see the full face and profile in each of the paintings?

Art Materials	
Paper	Container of water
Pencil and eraser	Newspaper (to cover work area)
Paints and brushes	

Learning Outcomes

1. Explain what Picasso tried to show with Cubism.

2. Explain what you did to distort the portrait you painted.

3. Tell whether you prefer distorted or realistic portraits, and why.

30 Imaginary Beasts

Observing and Thinking Creatively

For many centuries, artists all over the world have created pictures of imaginary beasts. One of the most famous is the unicorn, pictured below. This dazzling white pony had a goat's head and beard and feet, a lion's tail, and one horn growing out of his forehead exactly between his eyes. People during the Middle Ages believed this horn would ensure good health. Observe the picture closely. How do you think the unicorn feels chained inside the fence in the meadow? What about him makes you think so?

The second picture shows a carved figure in the shape of a dragon. Actually, this carved dragon is a musical instrument from Java called a metallophone. Observe the dragon's head closely. How would you describe his expression or mood? Would you like to play this instrument?

In the middle of the 1500s, an artist in Persia painted the Rhino Wolf pictured here. It was an illustration for a legend from the Shah Namah about the ancient kings of Persia. What parts of the creature look like a rhino? What parts look like a wolf? Are there parts that look like any other animal? Observe the Rhino Wolf carefully. What kind of mood is it in? What makes you think so?

In this lesson you will create an imaginary animal and paint it. You will increase your awareness of the **anatomy** of animals, and you will show the **mood** of your creature with lines, color, and brushstrokes.

Franco-Flemish, The Hunt of the Unicorn, VII, The Unicorn in Captivity, *detail from tapestry. Metropolitan Museum of Art, New York.*

Oceanic-Java, Saron, *carved in the shape of a dragon. XIX century. Wood and metal, 36" × 15" × 48", slabs: 15½" to 13". The Metropolitan Museum of Art, The Crosby Brown Collection of Musical Instruments, 1889.*

Rhino Wolf. *Detail of* Bahram Gur Slays the Rhino Wolf, *miniature from Firdowsi:* Shah-nameh (Book of Kings). *Made for Shah Tahmasp (reigned 1524-76). Metropolitan Museum of Art, New York. Gift of Arthur A. Houghton, Jr., 1970.84*

Instructions for Creating Art

1. First, imagine an animal you would like to create. You might decide to combine parts of insects with elephants or horses with snakes. You may wish to draw your own version of the Lochness Monster, Big Foot, or another creature described in legends or stories. Explore your imagination!

2. Now practice drawing body parts using techniques you have learned in previous lessons. Notice how the artist of the Rhino Wolf joined the horns to its head. He showed the base of the horn as part of a circle and painted it a different color from the head. Practice combining animal parts to create your imaginary beast. Then draw the beast you imagine.

3. Next, paint your creature. Use color, line, and brushstrokes to show mood. Is your beast gentle, mean, thoughtful, or startled? Display your finished creature with others from your class.

Art Materials	
Drawing paper	Mixing tray
Pencil and eraser	Container of water
Paints and brushes	Paper towels

Learning Outcomes

1. Name three examples of imaginary beasts and tell something unusual about each.

2. Describe the mood of your beast, and describe what you did to communicate this mood.

3. Give your beast a name, and tell a story about it.

Exploring Art

A Mythical Zoo

Imagine that you are a designer for a new movie being filmed in your city. The director has asked you to create a lifelike insect or animal with movable parts. You may create any kind of real or imaginary creature that you wish.

First, look through encyclopedias, science books, or nature books for pictures of creatures, animals, or insects similar to the creature you wish to create. Note where the limbs come out from the body and where joints are in the legs, neck, and torso. Study overall shape, proportions, color, and texture. Now draw a sketch of your creature. Use your imaginary beast design from Lesson 30 if you wish.

Next, select an empty container, such as a plastic bottle or small box, for the basic form, or **armature**. Bend, cut, or twist it into a basic body shape. Use wire or cardboard to form legs, wings, and other body parts. Attach these parts to the body with wire so that they can move. A trunk can be made with a long wire that goes through the animal's body.

Cover your creature with five or six layers of **papier-mâché**, small strips of paper dipped in wheat paste. Allow the sculpture to dry between layers. Mold bulges or muscles with additional papier-mâché. For the final layer, use very small pieces of paper towel to make a smooth surface.

When the papier-mâché is dry, sketch details on the body with a pencil. Study pictures of animals and insects for ideas for details and textures. Then paint the entire body with tempera paint. When the paint is dry, coat your creature with a layer of clear laquer to protect and strengthen it.

When your creature is complete, write a movie scene in which your creature has the leading role. Invent a name for it, and tell where it lives and what it eats.

Review

Using What You Have Learned

The Seine at Lavacourt was painted by French artist Claude Monet in 1880. Monet was very interested in the effect of light on **form**. Notice how the water seems to shimmer with reflected light. Apply some of the art ideas you learned in this unit as you examine this painting.

Claude Monet, The Seine at Lavacourt, *1880, oil on canvas, 38¾" × 58¾". Dallas Museum of Art, Munger Fund.*

1. Look at the brushstrokes in this painting. What do you notice about them? What is the name of the style of art shown here?
2. Monet achieved a feeling of **unity** in the way he used color in his work. What are the main colors he used, and where are these colors repeated?
3. Point out places in the painting where **tints** and **shades** are used.
4. What time of day is portrayed in this scene? What makes you think so? Identify the **horizon** in this picture.
5. What is the **center of interest** here? What leads your eye to it?
6. How do Monet's **reflections** differ from the objects they reflect? What feeling do you get from this painting? Explain why you feel this way.

Unit 3
Living with Art

Because Egyptians recorded their history in picture writing, or **hieroglyphics**, wall paintings, relief carvings, temples, and sculpture, we know much about their daily life and beliefs. Much of Egyptian art is related to the tombs—burial places of important leaders. These tombs were protected within **pyramids**, huge mountains of precisely cut stone. Walls were painted and beautiful sculptures were placed in the tombs to make the deceased person comfortable in his life in the afterworld.

Egyptians believed that the spirit had a life after death if images of the person, servants, food, wealth, and other practical necessities were preserved in a tomb. Many of the great pharaohs' tombs have been robbed because of the golden splendor inside.

One of the greatest archaeological finds was the tomb of King Tutankhamen, King "Tut," who ascended the throne when approximately nine years old in 1334 B.C. Discovered in 1922, this tomb was filled with ceremonial beds, thrones, vases, chariots, inlaid boxes, statues, weapons, and other objects that would bring luxury and comfort to the pharaoh in his afterlife. The solid gold mask shown here was placed over the head and shoulders of Tutankhamen's mummy and represents a likeness of the king, who died about age eighteen.

Egypt, Detail of funerary mask of Tutankhamen.

Egypt; Offering Bearer *(from tomb of Mekutra), Middle Kingdom, Dynasty II (c. 2009-1998 B.C.), painted wood, 44⅛"(h). Excavations of The Metropolitan Museum of Art, 1919-20; Rogers Fund and Edward S. Harkness Gift, 1920.*

Egypt, Sphinx of Amenhotep III *(below), XVIII Dynasty (1417-1379) B.C.), faience, 9⅞" x 5¼". The Metropolitan Museum of Art, Purchase, Lila Acheson Wallace Gift, 1972.*

Notice the blue *Sphinx of Amenhotep III.* A sphinx was a mythical creature with the head of a man, usually with the face resembling the pharaoh of the time, and the body, legs, and tail of a lion. The sphinx here has been given the facial features of Amenhotep III and guarded his tomb's entrance.

Art can reveal much about the beliefs and habits of individual cultures. In this unit, you will make art from many cultures.

31 The Art of Appliqué

Observing and Thinking Creatively

Have you ever fastened a patch to a jacket or sweater? Perhaps the patch represented an award for an accomplishment, or maybe it was a decoration. Fastening pieces of fabric to another material is called **appliqué**.

People all over the world use appliqué to decorate their clothes and other items. The Cuna Indians of Central and South America make appliqué designs called **molas**. First, several layers of cloth are sewn together. Then the top layers are cut and turned under to show the colors underneath. This is called **reverse appliqué**. Why do you suppose this process has this name?

Contemporary artists also use appliqué to make pictures. California artist Nancy Freeman uses many kinds of fabrics to add **pattern** to her appliqués. She shows markets, street scenes, and homes in many of her pieces of art.

In this lesson, you will make a paper mola similar to the Cuna Indian designs. Your mola will show bright colors and original designs.

Nancy Freeman, The Fish Market, Contemporary applique. Reproduced with permission of Lee Hanson.

Instructions for Creating Art

1. Sketch a large, very simple object, animal, or human shape on a brightly colored piece of paper.

2. Next, cut out the shape. Lay it down on another color of paper and trace around it, making your outline ¼ to ⅜ inches bigger all around than the original shape. Cut out this shape.

3. Use the second shape and another color of paper to make a third cutout shape that is a little bigger than the second one. Paste the three shapes together so that the smaller one is on top and the edges of the two larger shapes can be seen all the way around.

4. Paste the shapes on a rectangular piece of colored paper. Decorate the shapes and the background with cutout pieces of colored paper.

Art Materials	
Sketch paper	Scissors
Colored paper, 12″ × 18″ size	Paste
Pencil and eraser	

Learning Outcomes

1. Explain the difference between an *appliqué* and a *mola*.

2. Describe how you created your paper mola.

3. Of the appliqués shown here, which shows the best composition? Why?

71

32 Circular Weaving

Observing and Thinking Creatively

The **craft** of weaving has been practiced throughout the world for thousands of years. Ancient wall-paintings show us that the Egyptians had mastered weaving in 5,000 B.C.

At first, all weaving was done by hand. People used grasses, leaves, and even thin strips of wood to weave baskets, hats, and other articles. It took many hours to **spin** or twist fibers together to make blankets, clothing, and rugs.

All weavings have two sets of threads. One set, called the **warp**, stretches across a **loom**, or frame. The weaver repeatedly passes colored threads called the **weft** over and under the warp. By changing the weft threads, a weaver can create a great **variety** of shapes and patterns.

The first power loom was invented over 200 years ago. The cost of making cloth decreased, and people could afford to buy cloth and other things woven on power looms instead of making it themselves.

Although handweaving is still done in some parts of the world, it has become an artistic craft. Artists exhibit their **fiber art** at **galleries** and **museums**.

In this lesson, you will use your imagination to make an attractive, decorative weaving on a circular frame.

LaRene McGregor, circle weaving. Courtesy of the artist.

72

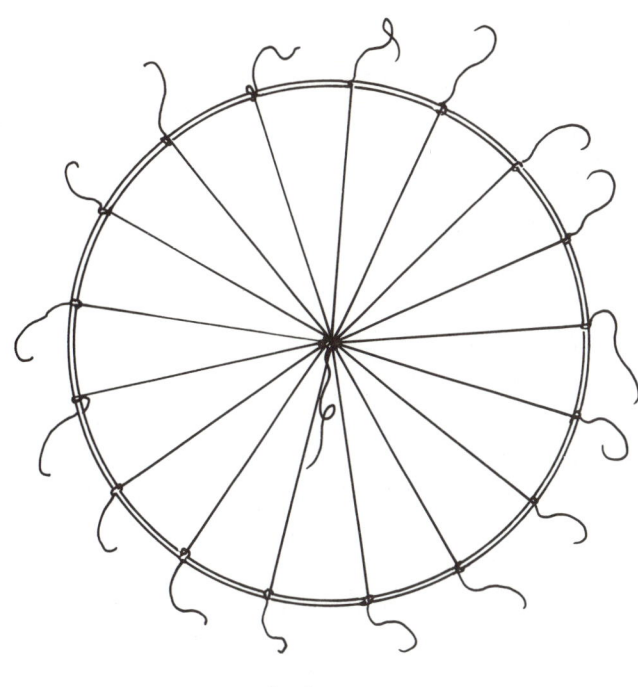

Circle Loom

Instructions for Creating Art

1. Bend a wire clothes hanger into a circle. If you prefer, you can bend a thin branch and tie it so that it is circular.

2. Cut eight strings that are at least six inches longer than the distance across the circular frame. Tie the ends to the frame so that each string stretches across the circle and passes through the center. Your frame should look like the illustration here.

3. Cut a separate string and tie it to the **center** so that it stretches across half the circle to the outside edge. This will give you an odd number of strings.

4. Make up little balls of colored yarn. Tie one end of one of the yarn balls to the center. Weave the colored yarn in and out, over and under, around and around the circle. Tighten the yarn as you work.

5. Colors can be changed by tying the end of the new yarn to the piece you have been using. You can also change direction by going back the way you started, or by going back and forth over and under just a few of the warp strings.

6. You may wish to add shells, bark, or other objects to your weaving design.

Art Materials

Wire hanger, hoop, or thin branch

String

Scissors

Colored yarns

Glue

Shells or other objects

THINK SAFETY

Learning Outcomes

1. Name and describe the main parts of a weaving.

2. Describe the specific features of your weaving.

3. Which weaving shown in this lesson is most similar to your weaving? Describe what is unique about your weaving.

73

33 Bark Cloth Designs

Observing and Thinking Creatively

What words would you choose to describe the texture of tree bark? Depending on the kind of tree, you might think of twisted, bumpy, or smooth. Wearing clothing made of bark might not seem like a good idea.

People who live in Africa, New Zealand, Hawaii, and also the Fiji Islands have used bark to make cloth similar to that shown here. This kind of cloth, called tapa, is made by taking the white inner fibers from the bark and beating them together into a fine, white cloth. To make the cloth more attractive, designs are added to it. Even though the African, Fijian, Hawaiian, and New Zealand cultures are separated by thousands of miles, their designs are similar.

There are seven symbols that are found in patterns created all over the world. They are called **universal symbols** because they are found in so many cultures. Look at the illustration of these symbols. How many can you find in the bark cloth samples shown here?

In this lesson, you will make a geometric design on softened paper that is very similar to bark cloth.

Tapa cloth. *From the Bishop Museum, Hawaii. Courtesy Anne G. Allen, San Diego State University Art Department.*

74

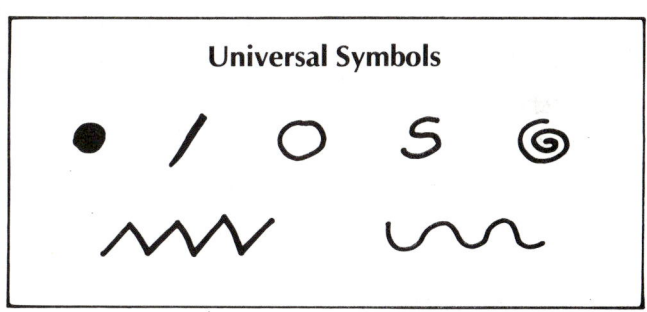

Instructions for Creating Art

1. First, cut out a large, seamless piece of paper from a large brown grocery sack. Now wad the paper into a tight ball and then smooth it out. Repeat this process until the paper is very soft and pliable.

2. Think about the symbols and pattern you will use in your design. You may want to divide the paper into boxes and strips and fill them with patterns of triangles, squares, and circles.

3. Make your geometric designs with brown and black crayons. You may wish to add a little white and orange to your design. Leave some of the shapes empty, and fill others with color.

4. When you finish your design, have a classmate identify the universal symbols you included. How many symbols did you use? Which symbol did you use most?

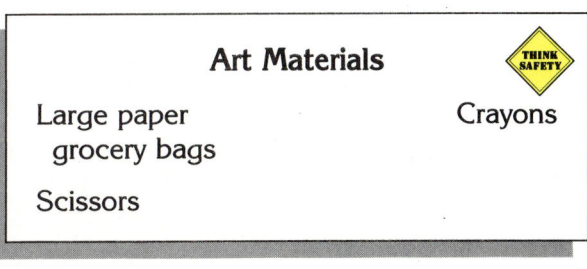

Learning Outcomes

1. Draw five of the seven universal symbols without looking at the ones shown here.

2. List the shapes you repeated to create pattern in your design. Which ones were empty and which ones were filled?

3. How is your design similar to those shown in the lesson? How is it different?

75

34 Mosaic Art

Observing and Thinking Creatively

The Byzantine Empire began in A.D. 323, when the first Christian Roman Emperor, Constantine, moved the capital of the Roman Empire away from Rome. The new capital was the Greek city of Byzantium, which Constantine renamed "Constantinople" after himself. Today this city is called Istanbul.

Christianity became the official religion of the Byzantine Empire. The churches built by Constantine and later emperors were stone buildings designed like a Greek cross, with four equal arms and a dome. Inside, the walls and even the dome were decorated with huge, colorful **mosaics**. Tiny bits of glass, gold, and stone, called **tesserae**, were imbedded in plaster to make pictures of religious and political figures.

Notice the bright, intricate designs in the mosaic of the Roman Emperor Justinian and the members of his court. This glittering portrait, made for a church in Ravenna, Italy, about A.D. 547, is a Byzantine mosaic.

The art form of mosaics had its beginnings in ancient Mesopotamia about 3,000 B.C. Mosaics often show scenes from events or stories and sometimes communicate messages. Most of the early mosaics depicted religious themes. Modern mosaics may picture the history or leaders of a city on the walls and interiors of public buildings.

In this lesson, you will create a mosaic made of paper tesserae to illustrate part of a myth, fable, legend, or story.

Court of Justinian. *Detail of an apse mosaic from the sanctuary of San Vitale, Ravenna, Italy.*

Instructions for Creating Art

1. Think of a myth, legend, fable, or story that you especially like. You may wish to look through books or ask your school librarian for ideas.

2. When you have a story idea in mind, use pencil to sketch the scene you would like to illustrate. Then choose the colors for your scene. Cut the colored paper into small pieces about one-fourth of an inch square.

3. Next, use chalk to sketch the outlines of your scene on black paper. Begin filling in the shapes with your little squares. You may cut your paper tesserae into smaller pieces to make them fit the shapes of your scene. Paste in the squares as you go along.

4. When your scene has been filled in with colored paper, stand back and look at it. Can you tell what is going on? You may wish to fill in the entire background of your mosaic.

5. Display your finished mosaic in your classroom. Can students guess what story you illustrated in your art?

Art Materials

Colored construction paper

Pencil and eraser

Light-colored chalk

Scissors

Paste

Old magazines (for pasting surface)

Learning Outcomes

1. Explain the meaning of the art terms *mosaic* and *tesserae*.

2. Identify the story you chose for your mosaic, and tell why you chose the particular scene you used in your design.

3. Which of the two fine art mosaics shown in this lesson do you think shows the best design? Give reasons for your choice.

77

35 Container Designs

Observing and Thinking Creatively

How many different containers have you used today? You may have poured milk and cereal from two types of containers into two others. You might have brought your books to school in a container.

Do you know that containers are one of the oldest, most widespread, and most versatile forms of art? Look at the **pre-Columbian** container on this page. This term is used with objects that existed in the Americas before the discovery by Columbus. This water vessel, shaped like an animal, was designed in Peru hundreds of years ago. Can you tell what kind of animal is represented?

The jar with the lid and two handles was made about 540 B.C. in Greece. A wedded couple is being greeted by a woman, while someone else plays a musical instrument. The boy in front of the horse will lead the wedding procession. The porcelain vase covered with bright and intricate designs was made about 300 years ago in China. Notice the details and the colors in the scene of the mother and child.

In this lesson, you will design your own original container. You may use a unique form, like the jaguar pitcher, paint a scene on it, or create an abstract design.

Peru, North Coast, Chavin, Vessel, stirrup spout, feline. VII-VI century B.C. Ceramic. 9 1/8"(h) × 5 5/8"(w) × 8 1/8"(d). The Metropolitan Museum of Art, The Michael C. Rockefeller Collection, Purchase, Nelson A. Rockefeller Gift, 1968.

Greek, ca. 540 B.C. Amphora with Cover: Marriage procession, perhaps of Herakles and Hebe. Ht. 18 1/2". The Metropolitan Museum of Art, Rogers Fund, 1917.

Chinese, Ch'ing Dynasty, K'ang Hsi Period (1662–1722). Porcelain Vase. Ht. 19¼". The Metropolitan Museum of Art, Bequest of John D. Rockefeller, Jr., 1960.

Instructions for Creating Art

1. Decide on the type of container you want to design. How would it be used? It may be practical, decorative, or both.

2. Study the containers in this lesson. Notice their **balance** and **shapes**, handles, lids, **color**, and the **lines** and **patterns** unique to each one. Make some practice sketches of ideas for your container. Then sketch your final container design on a sheet of art paper.

3. Use colored markers to color your design. You may want to use bright, **contrasting** colors, **analogous**, or closely related colors, or **tints** and **shades** of one color. Choose colors that will enhance the design and purpose of your container.

Art Materials

Drawing paper   Colored markers

Pencil and eraser

Learning Objectives

1. Name three uses for containers.

2. Describe special features of your container design.

3. How is your container like those shown in the lesson? How is it different?

36 Coil Pottery

Observing and Thinking Creatively

Have you ever made bird nests or long snakes by rolling clay or dough back and forth between your hands into thin strips? If you have, you have experienced one of the oldest ways of making pottery.

Clay **coils**, or long, snake-like strips, are easy to work with and can be used to create interesting effects in pottery. They can be smoothed to create a flat surface, or left in their round shape. Smaller coils can be used for adding details or decoration. Pots, flower vases, decorations, cookie jars, and plant holders can all be made of pottery.

In this lesson, you will use the clay coil method to build a bowl or pot. Your design may be **symmetrical**, having the same design all the way around, or **asymmetrical**, with different shapes or designs on opposite sides. If you like, you may use ideas from the container you designed in lesson 35.

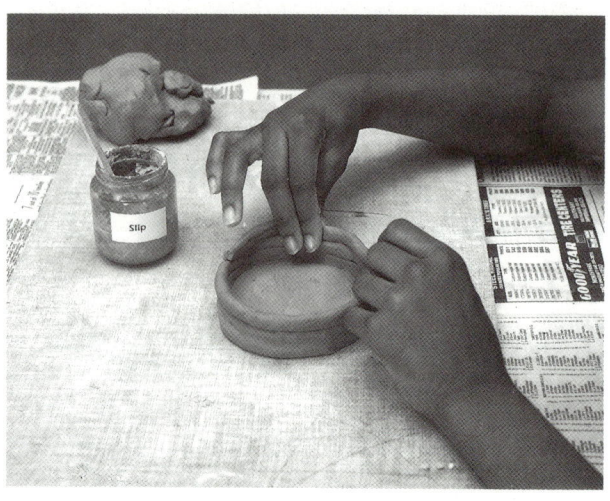

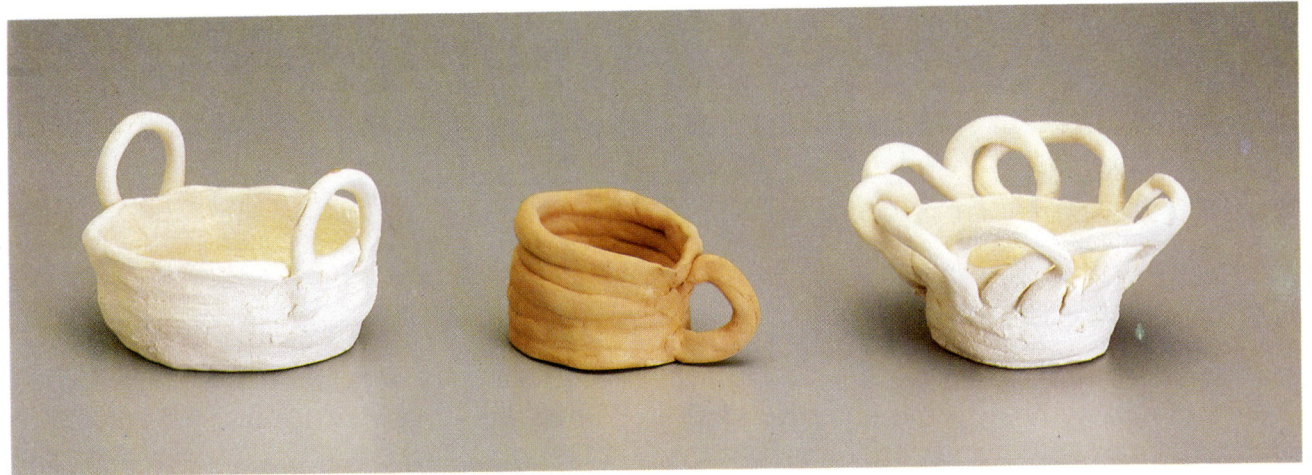

Instructions for Creating Art

1. First, think about a use for the pot you will make. Decide what the shape will be.

2. On a newspaper pad, press a lump of clay into a flat slab about a half-inch thick. Using a jar lid or another round object, mark a circle on the slab of clay. Use a knife to cut the circle and remove the extra clay. This circle may be used as the base of your bowl or pot. Clay pieces may be attached by first **scoring**, or roughening, the pieces. Then use **slip**, a creamy mixture of clay and water, to attach the coil to the base or to other coils. Smooth the joint with your finger.

3. Using your hands, roll a lump of clay into a long coil about one-half inch in diameter. Place the coil on the outside edge of the base to form a ring. Look at the picture in this lesson to see how this is done. Cut the coil so the ends meet, and then press the coil so that it sticks to the base.

4. Add more coils, joining each new coil to the previous one by scoring each coil and attaching it with slip. Then smooth the inside surface as much as possible with your fingertips. You may wish to smooth the outside also.

5. Handles, a lid, or decorations may be added with clay pieces. Texture may be created by scraping the outside with the flat edge of a key, plastic comb, fork, or another similar tool.

7. The clay is dry when it no longer feels cold to the touch. You can leave it as it is or **fire** it in a special oven, a **kiln**, which will make it stronger.

Art Materials	
Water-based clay	Comb, fork, key, etc. (for adding texture)
A 3- to 4-inch diameter jar lid	
Brush	Newspaper (to cover work area)
Paper towels	

Learning Outcomes

1. Explain the difference between *symmetrical* and *asymmetrical* balance.

2. Describe your pot design and tell what kind of balance you used.

3. Describe the best part of your pot and tell why you think that part is best.

37 The Human Figure in Action

Observing and Thinking Creatively

Representing human figures in action has been a part of art through the centuries. What do you suppose the first example might have been? Perhaps you have seen pictures of cave drawings that show a figure throwing a spear. The best way to learn to draw something is to actually look at the thing you are drawing. An artist must become aware of **proportions**, the relationship of the size of one part to another. Have you ever seen a drawing of a person that had one arm or leg longer than the other? Learning to measure proportions will make your drawings look more realistic.

It is a good idea to draw the basic shape of a thing and then fill in the details. When human figures are being drawn, it may be helpful to draw a simple line "skeleton" to make sure proportions are accurate and that the curves and angles of the arms and legs are correct.

Observe the position of Degas' *Ballerina*. Notice how the arms, legs, feet, and hands bend. Drawing sketches of a model who turns his or her arms, legs, hands, head, and torso every possible way will help you learn how bodies move.

In this lesson, you will draw a human figure in action. You will increase your awareness of how bodies move, body proportions, and how clothes affect body shape.

Edgar Degas, Ballerina, *Courtesy of the San Diego Museum of Art.*

Instructions for Creating Art

1. Choose a partner and decide who will model first. The first model should take an action position. The second student should then quickly sketch the outline of the model's pose. Check to see that the **proportions** look accurate. How wide are the shoulders? How long are the arms and legs? When the first sketch has been completed, change places.

2. When you have made your penciled outline, decide which body parts are hidden by arms and which parts overlap. Draw in the lines which separate parts.

3. Look at the **color** and **texture** of the clothing of the student you drew. Have the student assume the original pose again and see how the clothing looks. Sketch in the student's clothing. If the student is pretending to hold something in the pose, such as a ball, tool, or other object, add that to your picture.

4. Now, color your picture with the **medium** of your choice. Display your finished picture with others in your class. All the figures could be cut out, grouped together, overlapped to form a group **mural**. How many people can you recognize from these pictures?

Art Materials

12" × 18" white construction paper

Pencil and eraser

Scissors

Choice of media: Paints and brushes, colored markers, crayons, etc.

Learning Outcomes

1. What is the meaning of *proportion*?

2. Explain how you showed the texture and effects of clothing in your drawing.

3. How does your drawing show the feeling of action?

38 Relief Sculpture

Observing and Thinking Creatively

For thousands of years sculptors have carved or modeled **relief sculptures**, forms that rise up from a flat background. Peoples of the Stone Age carved or scratched figure designs in relief. Temples and palaces of the Egyptians, Greeks, and Assyrians were decorated with relief sculpture. Can you think of a modern example of a relief sculpture that you probably have with you right now? You may not think of *coins* as examples of relief sculpture, but they are.

This type of sculpture is often referred to by its name in French, **bas relief**. Depending upon how far out the form extends, it may be called **high relief**, **middle relief**, or **low relief**. High relief portrays figures projecting more than halfway from the background. Bas relief has been called sculpture drawing. The sculptor must be able to draw the outline of the subject accurately and in **proportion**. Look at the sculpture *Singing Boys*. It is a combination of high and low relief carved by American sculptor Herbert Adams in 1894.

Examine the Greek gravestone marker of a girl with pigeons, carved about 450 B.C. How old does she appear to be? Notice the quiet pose and serious mood of the child. What kind of relief does this look like to you?

In this lesson, you will draw a human figure and then carve a relief sculpture of it.

Greek, 5th Century B.C. Sculpture Reliefs. Grave Relief: Girl with Pigeons, *Parian marble, 31½″ × 15⅜″. From the Island of Paros. The Metropolitan Museum of Art, Fletcher Fund, 1927.*

Herbert Adams, Singing Boys, *relief, marble. The Metropolitan Museum of Art, Bequest of Charles W. Gould, 1932. (32.62.2)*

Instructions for Creating Art

1. Have a classmate model and sketch the form from several different angles. Look at the proportions of the person as you draw. How long are the arms in comparison with the legs? How long is the neck? Sketch the outline of the body first, and then go back and fill in other details.

2. When you draw the face, look carefully at its shape. There are four suggested shapes for a face: square, triangular, round, and oval. Notice that eyes are located approximately halfway up the head. Ears are generally located on each side between the eyebrows and the nose.

3. Select the sketch you like best for your relief sculpture. Next, roll out a slab of clay about half an inch thick. Use a pencil to carefully scratch the outline of your drawing into the smooth clay surface. Then begin carving away from the figure, creating a relief.

4. Now add small bits of clay to the high points of your figure, building up the different surface levels. Use a flat wooden tool to define the various planes of your relief figure, then gently smooth the edges. Add details and finish leveling the background to complete your sculpture.

Art Materials	
Paper	Clay carving tools such as old toothbrush, popsicle stick, etc.
Pencil and eraser	
Clay (oil or water-based)	

Learning Outcomes

1. Explain the difference between a *high relief* and *low relief* sculpture.

2. What level of relief did you make? Explain how you achieved different levels in your sculpture.

3. What mood did you express in your relief sculpture?

85

39 Costume Design

Observing and Thinking Creatively

Besides talking and writing, how many ways of communicating can you name? People give and receive information in many different ways, including hand signs, touching, expressions, tone of voice, and gestures. Our choices reveal a great deal about us.

Look at the **portrait** by Baroque artist Hyacinth Rigaud. What can you tell about this boy from the clothing he wears? Notice the ermine robe, the velvet lining, and the silk slippers on his feet. Although he is young, his clothes communicate that he is a rich and powerful person. This is Louis XV, who became king of France at age five.

The colored pencil sketches show costumes worn by characters in a play. What do the costumes tell you? What differences do you see between the two costumes? Where are shapes and lines repeated to make a **pattern**? Manner of clothing can tell a lot about the climate, living conditions, time period, and place in society of the person wearing the clothes. In almost every case, individuals add a personal touch to any outfit.

There are several possible careers which involve designing clothing. Some artists design clothes for the public, some design costumes for plays and movies, and others design and illustrate clothing for imaginary characters in books. As these designers work, they consider the shape or **silhouette** of the clothing, fabric, and color.

In this lesson, you will design a costume and then draw a figure wearing the costume. You will increase your awareness of **lines** and **forms** and experiment with a variety of techniques to show **textures** and **details**.

Hyacinthe Rigaud, French, 1659–1743. Louis XV as a Child. Oil on canvas, 77" × 55½", The Metropolitan Museum of Art. Purchase, Bequest of Mary Wetmore Shively in memory of her husband, Henry L. Shively, M.D., 1960.

Instructions for Creating Art

1. First, think about the kind of costume you would like to design. Who will wear the clothing you create? It might be a person who lived in the past, someone who lives in the future, or someone who exists only in your imagination. Look through history books, storybooks, encyclopedias, and magazines for ideas. What information about your character will you reveal in the costume you design?

2. Make practice sketches of your design. Use lines and shading to show the drape, folds, and creases of the cloth. Add details such as cuffs, collars, lace, buttons, ties, sashes, or pleats. Will your design be one-piece, or will it have layers?

3. Now draw your costume on a figure. Remember to draw the figure with the correct proportions. Complete the costume with colored pencils and markers or crayons and a lead pencil. You may wish to use your costume ideas in the next lesson on making a rod puppet.

4. When your costumed figure design is finished, ask a classmate to tell you what information he or she can gain about the figure just from looking at the costume.

Art Materials

| Colored pencils and markers, or crayons | Drawing paper |
| | Pencil and eraser |

Learning Objectives

1. Name three messages that may be communicated by a person's clothing.

2. Describe any special details you added to decorate the costume you drew. What fabric did you portray in your drawing?

3. Describe the character of the person who would wear the costume you designed.

40 Puppets at Play

Observing and Thinking Creatively

For thousands of years people have enjoyed puppets. Puppet-like figures have been found in tombs and ruins in ancient Egypt, Greece, and Rome; in China, Turkey, Japan, Persia; and in North and South America. Puppet theaters all over the world have entertained people with plays of adventures and humor. Because puppets take the place of live actors, they can do outrageous things that live actors could never do, such as leaping wildly in the air. With puppets, even animals can speak. Can you name any puppets?

Puppets come in many shapes and sizes and may be controlled in different ways. The most common is the **hand puppet**, like those used in Punch and Judy shows, and the Muppets. A **marionette** has a complete body whose movements are controlled by strings or wires. A **rod puppet** is a movable figure controlled by rods or sticks, usually from below the stage.

Rod puppets are especially popular in Japan, China, and Russia. Japanese puppeteers wear black clothing and stand in front of a black curtain while they manipulate colorful rod puppets in dramas.

In this lesson, you will make a rod puppet with a face and a fabric body. Using your imagination, your puppet will take part in a classroom drama. You will increase your awareness of shapes and experiment with ways to join the movable parts of a rod puppet.

© 1979 Henson Associates, Inc. All rights reserved. Used by permission.

3. Next, put glue on the end of a stick and gently push it about halfway into the head. Then cut a small x in the center of a fabric square. Slip the cloth onto the stick and glue it close to the head. Let this dry.

4. Now stretch out the fabric and glue the end of another stick to the fabric. While this is drying, cut out a hand from felt or construction paper. Then glue the hand to the end of the stick.

5. Move the two sticks to see what movements your puppet can make. You may wish to add another stick and hand to the other side of the puppet.

6. Get together with a few classmates and make up a story for your puppets. You might also have them act out fairy tales that you narrate.

Instructions for Creating Art

1. First, decide what you want your puppet's face to look like and make some sketches. Will it be distorted, or a fantasy character? What type and color of hair will it have? You might want to use ideas from the costume you designed in lesson 39. Make your puppet unique.

2. Draw the features you decided to use on a piece of felt or construction paper, and then cut them out. Glue them onto a Styrofoam ball. What do you want to communicate about your puppet? You may wish to use beads, buttons, glitter, feathers, yarn, and other objects to decorate your puppet's head. Let these pieces dry.

Art Materials

Styrofoam balls	Scraps of felt
Fabric squares (Approx. 12" × 12")	Construction paper
Glue	Yarn, beads, sequins, feathers, etc. (for decoration)
Scissors	
Paper	
Pencil and eraser	

Learning Outcomes

1. Name three kinds of puppets and tell which is the most popular.

2. Describe what you did to make your puppet unique. What do those things reveal about the personality of your puppet?

3. Identify your favorite kind of puppet, and explain what you like about it.

41 Exteriors: One Point Perspective

Observing and Thinking Creatively

Do you know what an *exterior* is? Exterior refers to something that is outside. Can you name the term for something that is inside? Very often artists who draw a landscape or an exterior view need to show **depth**, the distance from front to back or top to bottom.

The feeling of **space**, or depth, can be shown in several ways. Objects can **overlap** other objects, so that one appears to be behind another. Distance can be shown by drawing objects in the distance much smaller than objects close to you. Distance can also be shown by drawing shadows of objects and by making faraway objects appear hazy.

Using lines to show depth is called **linear perspective**. Parallel straight lines go away from you until they seem to meet and disappear. The place where they seem to meet is the **vanishing point**. This point is on the **horizon** line, where earth and sky meet. It is sometimes called the eye-level line.

Look at Childe Hassam's picture, *Boston Common at Twilight*. Notice how the trees and posts are set in a line that goes to a point about one-third of the way into the picture. The line drawing shows how this perspective was achieved. Now look at Claude Monet's *Beach at Trouville*. Can you see how the ocean, boardwalk, fence, and buildings all aim toward a single vanishing point?

In this lesson, you will draw an exterior scene using one point perspective. You will increase your awareness of depth and your ability to work with a ruler.

Childe Hassam, Boston Common at Twilight, *oil on canvas, 42" × 60". Gift of Miss Maud E. Appleton. Courtesy, Museum of Fine Arts, Boston.*

Claude Monet, Beach at Trouville, 1872, Oil on Canvas, Wadsworth Atheneum, Hartford; the Ella Gallup Summer and Mary Catlin Summer Collection.

Instructions for Creating Art

1. Use a ruler to draw a line across the top part of your paper, about two or three inches from the top. In the center of the line, place a dot to represent the vanishing point. Using the ruler, draw two straight lines, one from each side at the bottom of your paper to the dot. Your sketch should look similar to the line drawing shown in the lesson.

2. Now, imagine that you are looking down a roadway, walk, or railroad that goes as far as you can see. Draw some objects along the sides of the roadway. Be sure to make the objects smaller as they appear farther down the road.

3. When you achieve a good feeling of distance, color your sketch. Color can also show distance. Objects which are closer are usually brighter, larger, and more detailed than those in the distance.

4. Display your one point perspective drawing with others from your class. Which ones show the feeling of distance best? Why are they better than others?

Art Materials	
Drawing paper	Paints and brushes, crayons, colored pencils or markers, or oil pastels
Pencil and eraser	
Ruler	

Learning Outcomes

1. Name three ways to show a feeling of *depth* in art.

2. Explain how you showed depth in your picture.

3. How are *Boston Common at Twilight* and *Beach at Trouville* similar? In what ways are they different?

42 Foil Relief Houses

Observing and Thinking Creatively

How many different kinds of homes have you lived in or observed? If you look at the three homes pictured here, you'll notice that each one looks different from the others. People living in different countries have developed a variety of building styles for their lifestyles. An **architect**, one who designs buildings, must be concerned with the practical, technical parts of the building as well as its beauty.

Before he or she can design a building, an architect must know where a building is to be placed and what its purpose is to be. What kinds of conditions would make it important to build a home on stilts? What is the basic shape of the hut? Building materials must also be suited to the climate where the home is to be built.

Unlike the hut, the Japanese building shown here is built in layers with a tiled roof and sliding doors. Room divisions are often made with rice paper partitions.

Notice the picture of a Victorian style house. How is it different from the other two houses pictured here? How many shapes can you find in this design? The **foil relief** house shown in the lesson was modeled in the Victorian style. Creating a model increases awareness of **detail**, **shape**, **line**, **balance**, and **unity**. The model maker must decide how to use **emphasis**—which parts of the house will be dominant, or more important, and which will be subordinate, or less important.

In this lesson, you will choose a house design and make a foil relief house.

Instructions for Creating Art

1. Look through photographs, magazines, books, or take a field trip to observe different styles of homes. You may wish to use a style of home found in another country. When you find a home you like, look for the simple shapes in the design. Draw the general outline of the structure. Then add windows, doors, and large details. You will be working with simple lines and basic shapes more than small details.

2. When your sketch is complete, draw it on a piece of chipboard or poster board. Use white glue to apply cut pieces of string, toothpicks, spaghetti, screen, macaroni, and similar items to outline the lines and shapes of your design. Build up parts of the design that are to stand out. Then let the structure dry thoroughly.

3. Now brush the entire surface of your design with watered-down white glue. Pull out a sheet of foil that extends about four inches longer than your board. Gently crumple the foil and then smooth it out. It should have lines and texture in it. Spread the foil over your relief design.

4. Next, use a soft cloth to rub over the foil to reveal the raised lines and shapes of your design. Fold the foil over the edges of the board, and tape them to the back.

5. Finally, very carefully brush ink over the surface of the foil. With a soft, dry cloth, rub off the excess. This will give your foil relief an antique, textured look.

Art Materials

Sketch paper	Ruler
Pencil and eraser	Scissors
Chipboard or poster board	Toothpicks, spaghetti, macaroni, string, screen, etc.
Aluminum foil	
Ink	Brush
Soft cloth	

Learning Outcomes

1. Name two things an architect must know before he or she can design a building.

2. Identify the shapes you included in your foil relief house. Tell how you created the different textures in your design.

3. Describe the house style you chose for your design, and tell why you chose it.

93

43 Greek and Roman Architecture Styles

Observing and Thinking Creatively

Have you ever seen a building that had tall columns in front? If so, you have seen a feature of Greek **architecture**. The ancient Greeks and Romans built many examples of beautiful architecture. They built temples, sports and entertainment stadiums, and elaborate arches. **Symmetry** in balance was important to both the Greeks and the Romans, so their buildings may have a similar look. But there are important differences between the two styles of architecture.

Notice the picture of the Parthenon below. This Greek temple was built about 440 B.C. to honor the Greek goddess Athena. It is an example of **Doric** architecture. Look at the **fluted**, or grooved, **columns**. Made of marble, each is massive, stumpy, and without a base. The column narrows toward the top. Carved statues decorate the **frieze**, the space just under the roof all the way around the temple. Do you notice any curves in this Greek building design?

Now examine the Roman Arch of Constantine and the Colosseum. The Romans invented a form of concrete and were able to form curved arches. What other similarities and differences between Greek and Roman styles can you find?

In this lesson, you will design and draw a building that combines features from both Greek and Roman architecture styles. You will increase your awareness of structure and experiment with a variety of lines and details to show style, balance, and beauty in your building design.

Parthenon. Athens, Greece

Arch of Constantine. Rome, Italy.

Colosseum. Rome, Italy.

Instructions for Creating Art

1. Carefully study pictures of Greek and Roman architecture styles in this lesson, in encyclopedias, and in other books. Observe the features and details of these styles. What parts appeal to you most?

2. Before you sketch your building, decide what its purpose is to be. Will it be used as a sports stadium? Is it to be a home? Is it to be an arch honoring the achievement of someone or a special group? When you have a purpose in mind, draw some practice sketches of a building that combines features from both Greek and Roman architecture. Remember that the design must be balanced symmetrically.

3. Make a finished drawing of your building. You may wish to go over your drawing very carefully in ink. Label your building and display your architectural design in your classroom.

Art Materials

Drawing paper

Pencil and eraser

Ink and pen or marking pens

Learning Outcomes

1. Name two similarities and two differences between Greek and Roman styles of architecture.

2. Identify the Greek and Roman features of your building design.

3. Tell which you prefer, Greek or Roman architecture styles, and why.

44 Towers and Turrets

Observing and Thinking Creatively

Observe the four structures in this lesson. What do they have in common? Although they were built in Russia, the United States, Germany, and Malaysia, they all feature **towers** or **turrets** in their **architectural** design. A tower is a tall, vertical structure which either stands free or is a part of a building. A turret is just a small tower that usually contains stairs and is located at the top of a building.

Russian architects used the **dome** design in the roofs of many of their cathedrals. Their designs included pointed domes and slanted, rather than flat, roofs. Why do you think these designs were appropriate for a country with heavy snowfall?

Towers were also used in castles. How many towers can you find in the German castle? Impressive towers communicated the importance of the persons who live there.

In a country which has neither kings nor queens, a sand castle like "Sleeping Beauty's Castle" is a fantasy creation. It looks like something magical from a fairy tale. In Europe, however, towers were real and were used as a part of the castle's defense. From their high perch, lookouts could spy enemies approaching in the distance. Prisoners could also be kept isolated in the towers. For the people who lived near the castle, the towers were a symbol of safety.

Look at the tower in Malaysia. How is it similar to the other structures shown here?

In this lesson, you will design and color a building that has towers and turrets. You will increase your awareness of building structure and exercise your imagination as you use a variety of **lines**, **shapes**, **form**, and **details** in your original architectural design.

St. Basil's Cathedral, *Moscow*

Sleeping Beauty's Castle, *San Diego, California*

Neuschwanstein Castle, *Germany*

Kasho Kumagi, *Malaysia*

Instructions for Creating Art

1. Study structures that feature towers and turrets by looking through books and magazines or going on a field trip. What sort of tower do you especially like? Think about the purpose of your building. It may be a fantasy structure, or a modern building, such as a library, or perhaps a bell tower or fort. Think about the location of your building and what purpose the turrets or towers might have.

2. Make practice sketches of your building design. Experiment with placing the towers in different places on your building. When you like the balance of your design, draw it on another piece of paper.

3. Add details such as windows, moats, doors, walls, or patterned roof designs. Think about what materials might be used in constructing your building. Would it be made of marble, stone, wood, tile, plaster, adobe, logs, metal, or something else? What colors might be used?

4. Color your completed drawing. You may wish to add landscaping details such as trees, walkways, shrubbery, or flowers. Display your finished architectural design. If you wish, construct your design with boxes, paper tubes, cardboard cutouts, and so on.

Art Materials

Drawing paper

Pencil and eraser

Colored markers, chalk, oil pastels, crayons, colored pencils, etc.

Paper boxes, tubes, etc. for construction

Glue

Scissors

Learning Outcomes

1. Define *tower* and *turret*.

2. Describe special features of your building, and name its purpose. What did you try to communicate with your design?

3. Which of the structure styles shown in this lesson do you like best? Why?

45 Monuments of the World

Observing and Thinking Creatively

Have you ever visited a **monument**? A monument is a building, statue, or other structure built in remembrance and honor of an important person or event.

One of the most beautiful monuments in the world is the Taj Mahal in India. Emperor Shah Jahan had this building designed and constructed after the death of his beloved wife, Mumtaz Mahal, in 1629. The empress is buried in a vault beneath the center room.

Another type of monument is this Pioneer Handcart, located in Salt Lake City, Utah. In 1856, almost 2,000 pioneers walked 1,200 miles from Iowa to the Salt Lake Valley. All of their possessions were carried in small, two-wheeled handcarts. This monument was built to honor and remember the courage of those pioneers.

A tall column topped by a spectacular gold angel rises out of one of the busiest streets in Mexico City, Mexico. It is called the Column of Independence. Statues representing law, justice, war, and peace stand at its base. This monument recognizes Mexico's independence from French rule in 1867.

Love, heroism, and national spirit are only a few of the reasons monuments have been built throughout history. How many monuments can you name? In this lesson, you will design and make your own monument.

Taj Mahal, *India, Air India Library, Courtesy Information Service of India, Embassy of India, Washington, D.C.*

Pioneer Handcart Monument, *Salt Lake City, Utah*

Column of Independence, *Mexico City*

Instructions for Creating Art

1. Think of something that is important to you. It might be a person, a special day in your life, a holiday or day in history, or something you believe in. When you have an idea, make some sketches of possible designs for your monument. You may want to show a real object, or you can use **symbols** that stand for an idea. Observe the **composition** of each of the monuments shown in this lesson.

2. Decide on one design, and draw it on a large piece of paper. It should show **unity** of theme, but also include a **variety** of shapes. Then you can paint, carve, model, or sculpt your finished design. The medium you choose should fit the theme of the monument you designed.

3. Display your finished monument with others from your class.

Art Materials

White paper

Pencil and eraser

Your choice of materials

THINK SAFETY

Learning Outcomes

1. Name two monuments and two reasons for building monuments.

2. Describe how you achieved both unity and variety in your monument.

3. Explain how your monument honors or represents something important to you.

Exploring Art

Who Lived in This Place?

What must an **architect** consider when a building is to be designed? He or she must plan **shapes**, **colors**, surfaces, **textures**, materials, and **space** according to the purpose of the building. Perhaps you have seen an architect's model, a miniature **replica** used to show clients how the completed building will look. Lifelike details and sculptured figures are often included with these models to make the building look more realistic.

For this activity, you will create a **diorama**, a two- and three-dimensional miniature scene of a room. This is to be a room or place used or lived in by a person or character from history or from literature. Think of people such as Abraham Lincoln, Clara Barton, Cleopatra, characters from *The Lion, the Witch, and the Wardrobe, The Black Cauldron,* or inventors. You will add details that give clues about the time period and person whose room or place you have chosen to create. What objects, furniture, and decorations would be found there? One diorama below shows the garden discovered by Mary Lennox in *The Secret Garden.*

When you have a person in mind, begin making your diorama. You may cut away the top and one side of a box, such as a laundry soap or shoe box. Decide where windows, doors, and furnishings will be placed. You may wish to paint in some of the details of your room. If your room has a rug, cut a piece of material in the desired shape and place it on the "floor" of the box. Plan and make furniture that might have been used by your character with folded cardboard, balsa wood, or objects glued together and painted. As you work, keep in mind correct proportions. Is the chair as large as the bed? Make sure that the furnishings fit the time period when your character lived.

When the walls and furnishings are complete, add any details that indicate your character's special interests or activities. Whose room might have a tiny flag with a threaded needle inserted in it? Whose room might have log walls and a stovepipe hat on a table? Have your classmates guess who lived in the place you created from the special details you added.

Review

Using What You Have Learned

This bold, colorful building design is the Central Library of the National Autonomous University of Mexico. Artist Juan O'Gorman used about 7-1/2 million stones or **tesserae** to make this mural. He covered the outside of this ten-story building with pictures of the people and **symbols** of his country.

1. O'Gorman traced Mexican history from prehistoric times to the present. The sun and animals were popular symbols. Where can you find examples of the sun and animals in this mural?
2. Did the artist use mainly **primary colors** or **earth colors** in his design? What makes you think so?
3. Looking at the building from the front, what is the **center of interest**? How can you identify the center of interest?
4. What type of **art form** is the design for this building?
5. Do you think the artist successfully used the **elements** and **principles of art** to communicate his theme? Why or why not?

Unit 4
Communicating Through Art

Diego Rivera, Flower Day, 1925, Oil on canvas, 58" x 47½". Los Angeles County Museum of Art, Los Angeles County Fund.

Since the days of the ancient Indian civilizations, the arts of Mexico have fulfilled spiritual as well as practical needs. The architecture of the Mayan and Toltec Indians was related mainly to religion. These ancient Indians painted **murals** of scenes from their day-to-day lives and their ideas of the afterlife on the walls of temples and pyramids.

The Aztecs loved crafts and beautiful things. When Spanish explorer Hernando Cortes discovered the Aztec empire, he found handicrafts of silver, gold, precious stones, embroidered cloth, and pottery in a thousand shapes. The Aztecs worshipped the sun with human sacrifices. They communicated their traditions and beliefs with **symbols** in shape and color.

Following the Spanish Conquest, there was a blending of Indian and Spanish art styles. Mexican architecture was influenced by the Spanish missions. Spain dominated Mexico until 1821, when Mexico gained her independence. Muralists such as Diego Rivera, Jose Orozco, and David Siqueiros told the story of the revolution in murals.

In this unit, you will explore ways of communicating through art. You will use symbols, letters, illustrations, pictures, and your own unique perceptions to communicate your ideas.

46 Original Banners

Observing and Thinking Creatively

Picture in your mind a king's army marching into battle. In your imagination, you probably see knights or soldiers leading the troops and carrying large **banners** with special **symbols** on them representing their country.

What banners can you think of that are used today? How about the banners that are stretched across the street in front of marching bands? Similar banners are hung high above the street between light posts to announce events or to welcome visitors. Many sports teams have banners with special designs or pictures on them. Do you know what the stars and stripes on the United States' flag represent?

People who design and make flags are called **vexillographers** (vek-sə-läg-rə-fərz). Anders Holmquist became a vexillographer because he was fascinated with color, movement, and the feelings that come from watching a flag in the wind. He has designed flags and banners for a king, entertainers, artists, restaurants, parks, shopping malls, and public buildings. Look at *Wings* by Holmquist on this page. What do you think it was designed to represent?

In this lesson, you will design a banner that represents your achievements or something that is important to you.

Anders Holmquist, Wings.

Instructions for Creating Art

1. Think of **symbols** that represent your accomplishments or interests. Sketch a design for a banner using these symbols. Your banner shape may be a square, triangle, or an original shape that fits your theme, like *Wings*.

2. When you decide on a design, draw it on a large sheet of paper. Then you may either paint your drawing or make it from construction paper. Choose colors that suit you and enhance the meanings of your symbols. Will you use bright, contrasting, **complementary** colors, or **analogous** colors, from the same color family? Use color as well as design to make the symbols on your banner the **center of interest**.

3. Display your banner by hanging it up in your classroom. Be prepared to tell your class about the banner and what its design and colors represent.

Art Materials	
White paper	Pencil and eraser
Paints and brushes or colored construction paper	Scissors
	Glue

Learning Outcomes

1. Name three uses for *banners*.

2. Describe how you used color to enhance the meaning of your banner.

3. Tell how your *symbols* represent an idea, thing, or place.

105

47 A Monochrome Self-Portrait

Observing and Thinking Creatively

How can you tell what kind of mood a friend is in? You might notice tone of voice and the words your friend uses, but the first clue probably comes from the person's facial expressions. Half-closed eyes may tell us someone is feeling sleepy. Close-knit eyebrows and a tight smile might indicate anger. It has been said that the eyes are the mirror of the soul, and much can be learned from studying faces. What can you tell from the faces shown in this lesson?

When painting **portraits**, artists try to capture personality traits and mood as well as accurate **proportions** of facial features. An artist might use shading or color to communicate a mood. A particular feature might be emphasized by **distorting** lines or **highlighting**. A certain pose might reveal attitude, and interesting details might be added that relate to the portrait subject's occupation, hobbies, or life-style.

In this lesson, you will draw and paint a **monochrome**, or single color, self-portrait. You will select a color to be used with black, a pose, and a mood, that will communicate the essence of your personality.

106

Instructions for Creating Art

1. You may bring a picture of yourself or use a mirror. Think about the pose you wish to portray and what expression you want to emphasize. Will your portrait show your head, or the shoulders and head? What clothing will be shown?

2. When you have an idea of what you want to communicate, draw the outline of your head on a large piece of paper. Lightly draw in the shape of your hair. Notice how close together or far apart your eyes are. What shape is your nose? Observe the shape and size of your lips and ears. Study your face and lightly draw in the shapes of the dark and shadowed areas. Do not draw in details. Add clothing if you wish.

3. When your sketch is finished, choose a colored piece of paper for your portrait. Draw the outline of your head and paint it with a color that expresses your mood or personality. Paint the shape of your hair black. When the face has dried, sketch in the eyes, nose, and mouth. Fill them in with black paint or a black marker, keeping edges crisp and clean.

4. Display your finished artwork with others in your class.

Art Materials

Drawing paper
Pencil and eraser
Black marker
Paints and brushes
Mixing tray
Container of water
Paper towels
Newspaper (to cover work area)

Learning Outcomes

1. Name three things artists try to communicate in painting portraits.

2. Describe how you showed your personality in your self-portrait.

3. What does the color you chose for your portrait communicate about you?

48 A Personal Treasure Box

Observing and Thinking Creatively

Have you ever dreamed of finding a buried or sunken treasure? Before there were safety deposit boxes, banks, and safes, people put their jewels, gold, and other valuable possessions in trunks or boxes. These containers could be locked with a padlock and were small enough to be taken on journeys. Some were stolen or lost when a ship sank, and others were buried and never dug up again. Wouldn't it be exciting to find one?

In this lesson, you will use your imagination to design and create your own treasure box out of papier-mâché. You will cover your box with pictures that express your own unique personality. A work of art created by gluing bits of paper, photographs, or other materials to a flat surface is called a **collage**. You may wish to place something in your collage container that represents a treasure to you or that expresses your personality.

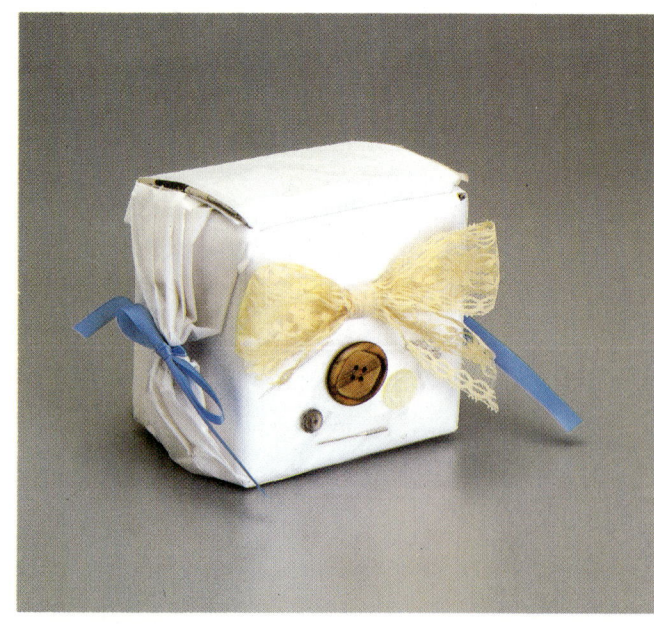

Instructions for Creating Art

1. Choose a small, empty container, such as a tin, cardboard box, or a bottle. It should have a wide opening and a lid.

2. Cover your desk with several layers of newspaper. Tear other newspapers into strips about two inches long and one inch wide. Dip the strips in papier-mâché paste, and use them to completely cover the outside of your container, with at least three layers. Let the papier-mâché covered container dry thoroughly.

3. Plan how you will decorate your box to express your personality. You may want to cover it with snapshots of you or of things that interest you. You may choose magazine pictures of items that represent your hobbies or interests. Or, you may paint your box with tempera paints. You may wish to paint symbols of achievements that are important to you. Use your imagination as you choose a theme and colors for your design.

4. When your box is decorated, you may want to coat the entire container with shellac or varnish, or acrylic spray to give it a clear, glossy finish. Then put something in the box that you treasure or that represents your personality. Be prepared to discuss your box with your class.

Art Materials

Small gift boxes, bottles with lids, or any other lightweight container	Newspaper
	Your choice of decorating materials
Wheat paste for papier-mâché	Shellac, varnish and brushes, or acrylic spray

Learning Outcomes

1. What does **collage** mean?

2. Describe how you expressed your personality with your box design.

3. What object or treasure did you put in your container? Why did you choose it?

49 Transformations and Illusions

Observing and Thinking Creatively

Transformation refers to the process of changing one thing into another. If you look carefully at the pictures shown here, you will see different ways of transforming or changing one thing into another.

First, look at the woodcut *Sky and Water I*, by M.C. Escher. In this scene, Escher worked with **positive**, or filled, and **negative**, or empty, **space**. The white fish which encircle the black birds form the sky they fly in, and the black birds form the water the fish swim in. Observe the changes in each level of fish. Combining two creatures that undergo transformation and fitting them together creates a fascinating **illusion**.

Now look at the design by Jean Gerard, who called himself "Grandeville." The transformation into a frog occurs with slight, consistent changes in the man's profile.

In this lesson, you will choose a person or a scene and transform it into something else. You will increase your awareness of the importance of detail and shape as you exercise your imagination.

M.C. Escher, Sky and Water I, 1938, woodcut, 17½" × 17¼". Courtesy CORDON ART, B.V., Holland.

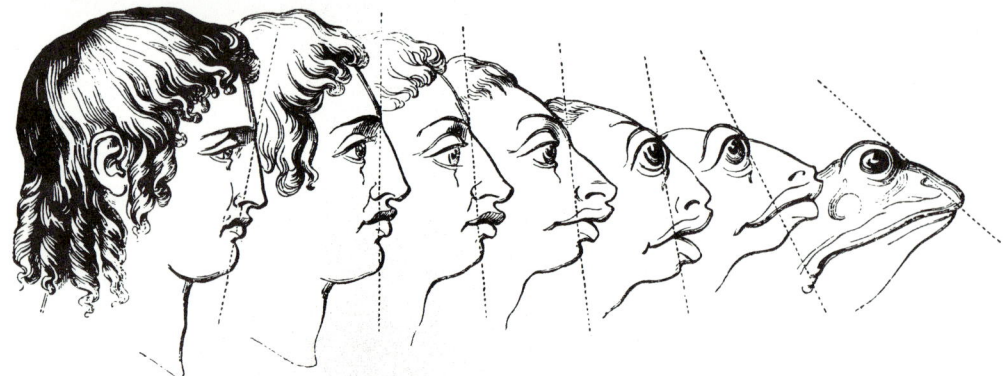

Grandeville, Heads of Men and Animals Compared, from Le Magasin Pittoresque, 1844. Reproduction courtesy of Atheneum Publishers, New York.

Instructions for Creating Art

1. First, decide what kind of transformation you would like to make. Then decide on a subject for your transformation. Observe the illustrations in this lesson to help you get ideas. Would you like to transform a plant? Perhaps you know someone whose facial features remind you of an animal. Or maybe you would like to make a **pattern** of shapes that fit together like Escher's *Sky and Water I*.

2. When you have decided on a subject, think about where you will place it on your paper. How many steps will your transformation take? Make practice sketches of your ideas to help you decide how to **compose** your picture and use **space**.

3. Draw your transformation. If you are doing a series, be consistent in keeping the basic sizes and shapes that do not change. Be aware of balance and details.

4. You may wish to color your drawing when it is finished. Did you make smooth transitions from one shape to another? Give your artwork a title and display it in your classroom.

Art Materials	
Drawing paper	Colored pencils and markers
Pencil and eraser	

Learning Outcomes

1. What does *transformation* mean?

2. Explain how you transformed one thing into another.

3. Which transformation in this lesson do you think is most skillfully done? Why do you think so?

50 Adventures in Perception

Observing and Thinking Creatively

M.C. Escher, an artist from The Netherlands who lived from 1898-1972, was fascinated with the structure of **space**. **Emphasis** on **height**, **depth**, and **distance** is characteristic of his work. He sometimes showed views of things from impossible angles, showing what is seen from above and what is seen from below at the same time.

Observe Escher's picture *Drawing Hands*. The right hand is sketching the left hand on the drawing paper. The hands look as if they have emerged from the paper to draw the cuffs. Notice how Escher's use of **shading**, **detail**, and **line** make the hands seem to be coming right out of the flat paper.

Now look at Escher's *Relativity*. How many illusions can you find in this picture? For another example of Escher's work see *Sky and Water I* in lesson 49.

The old Persian horse puzzle is a different kind of adventure in perception. If you look at it closely and turn the picture to one side, you can see four horses. Two horses are facing each other, with legs extended. Another view shows two horses back to back, with legs tucked in. Although two different views are possible, only two horses can be seen at any one time.

Puzzles and illusions take skill and imagination to create and can be very entertaining. In this lesson, you will design an illusion of your own. You will increase your awareness of space, **shape**, and detail as you create an unusual perception from your own mind.

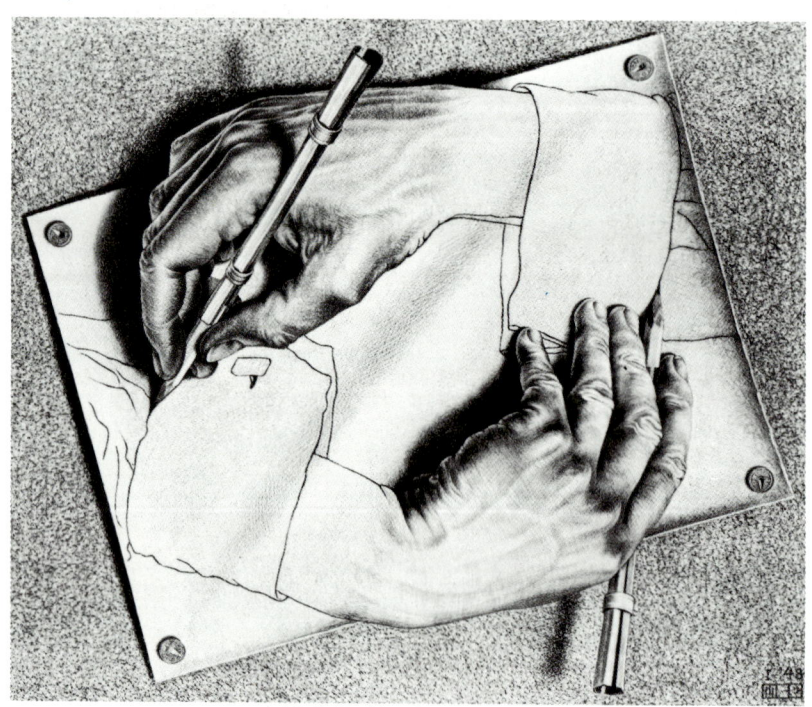

M.C. Escher, Drawing Hands, National Gallery of Art, Washington. Gift of Mr. C.V.S. Roosevelt.

M.C. Escher, Relativity, *National Gallery of Art, Washington. Gift of Mr. C.V.S. Roosevelt.*

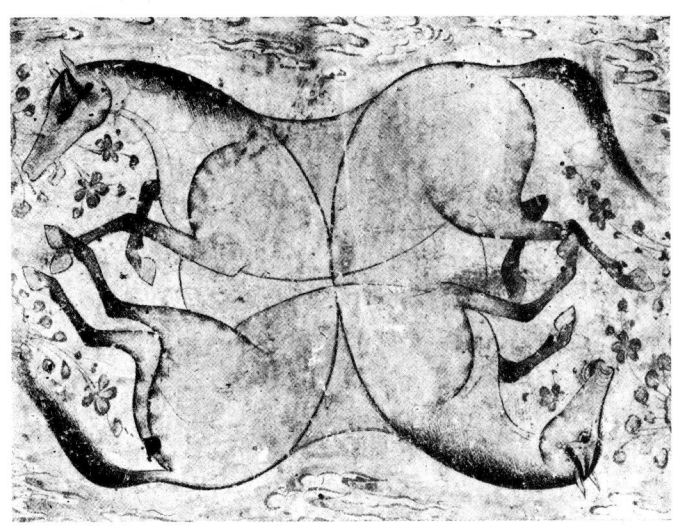

Persian, Four Horses Concentric Design, *17th century, ink on paper. Courtesy, Museum of Fine Arts, Boston. Francis Bartlett Donation of 1912 and Picture Fund.*

Instructions for Creating Art

1. Look through encyclopedias and other sources to see how artists have drawn illusions. Decide what type of illusion or puzzle you would like to draw. Perhaps you will draw a building with stairs that go nowhere. You might draw a puzzle similar to the Persian horses. Experiment with ideas until you find one you want to use.

2. Now, draw your illusion. Study the way Escher used shading and detail to make something appear realistic. If you draw a puzzle, you may wish to attach the parts in each view, like the Persian horse.

3. If you show depth, study Escher's technique of making the closest objects brighter, bigger, and more detailed than those which are behind. You may color your drawing if you wish.

4. Display your finished adventure in perception with others in your classroom. How is your artwork unique? What does it have in common with others on display?

Art Materials	
Drawing paper	Colored pencils, markers, chalk, or crayons
Pencil and eraser	

Learning Outcomes

1. Name two characteristics of M.C. Escher's artwork.

2. Describe the kind of illusion you chose to create and tell how you achieved it.

3. Which of the illusions shown in this lesson do you like best? Why?

51 Surrealism: A Dream Landscape

Observing and Thinking Creatively

Have you noticed how impossible things can happen in dreams? Perhaps you are flying like a bird, or things are upside down. Can you remember a dream where there were parts that were nothing like the real world?

A **movement** in art called **Surrealism** began in Paris in 1924. This art idea placed **emphasis** on images from the unconscious mind. The artist who painted in the surrealistic style made pictures that looked like scenes from an unreal, dream world.

Salvador Dali is a Surrealist who often transformed objects in his paintings and arranged them in unusual ways. His paintings are precise and almost **photographic**, but the objects may be **distorted** and shown in strange combinations.

René Magritte developed a humorous style of Surrealism by showing unlikely combinations of ordinary objects in his paintings. These paintings are very **realistic** in detail, but they often leave the viewer wondering about the artist's message.

In this lesson, you will create a landscape or seascape that shows a place that exists only in your imagination.

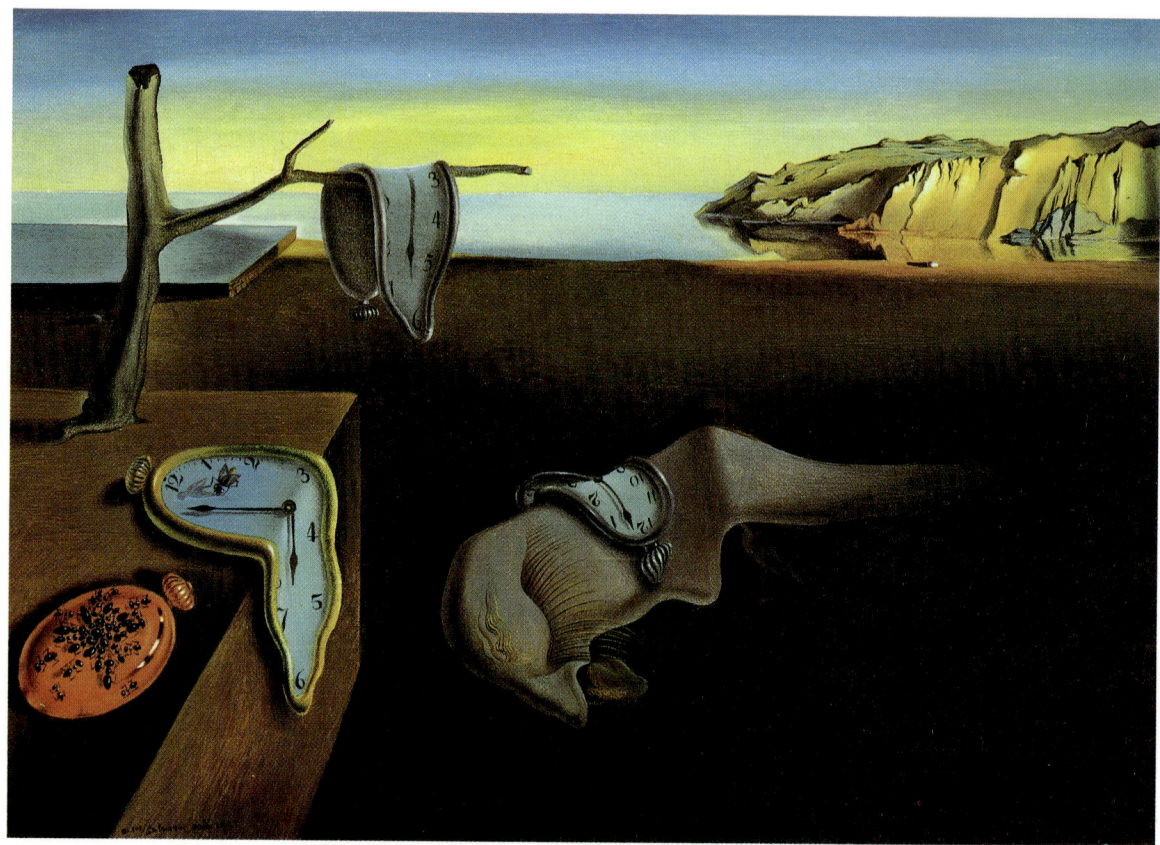

Salvador Dali, The Persistence of Memory, 1931, oil on canvas, 9½" × 13". Collection, The Museum of Modern Art, New York. Given anonymously.

René Magritte, Time Transfixed, 1939, Oil on canvas, 57½ × 38½ in., Courtesy of The Art Institute of Chicago, Joseph Winterbotham Fund.

Instructions for Creating Art

1. Sketch some ideas for a landscape or scene. Put in a **horizon** line that is above or below the middle of the page. Decide what objects or creatures you are going to put in your drawing.

2. Plan your fantasy scene so that the parts are well-balanced. Put in combinations of things that would be seen only in a dream. You may wish to **distort** objects, as Dali did in his picture.

3. Sketch your fantasy scene. Add color to your picture with colored markers. Display your finished landscape with others in your class.

Art Materials

White paper
Colored markers
Pencil and eraser

Learning Outcomes

1. Name two characteristics of *surrealistic* paintings.

2. Tell how you created a dream world in your art work.

3. Which of the paintings shown here do you like best? Why?

52 Positive and Negative Space

Observing and Thinking Creatively

Look at the two squares pictured in this lesson. Which looks larger? What makes it appear larger than the other? It is possible to create certain illusions with **shape** and **space** by simply changing the background. You have used this concept in earlier lessons. If you wanted to make yellow appear very vibrant and bright, what color background would you use? The **complement** of yellow is violet, and placing those colors together gives yellow a very bright appearance.

Space that is filled is called **positive space**, and space that is empty is called **negative space**. If you are a person who enjoys puzzles, you are probably an expert at recognizing positive and negative space shapes.

In this lesson, you will design a puzzle using positive and negative space. You may create a mirror image illusion with your shapes, or you may choose to arrange the pieces in another way.

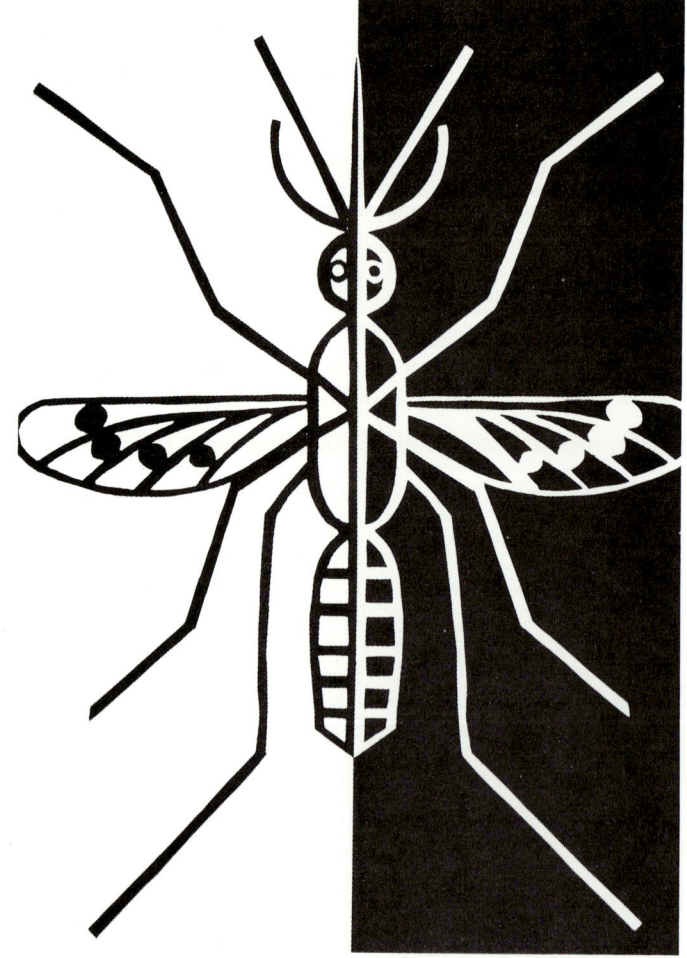

Instructions for Creating Art

1. First, sketch some interesting shapes on a piece of scratch paper. When you have seven or eight shapes that you like, choose two colors for your puzzle. Decide which color will provide the background, the negative space shapes. This sheet of paper must be twice as large as the other piece. Black and white or complementary colors will create dramatic effects.

2. Place the smaller sheet on top of the larger one. Draw your shape designs on the smaller sheet of paper. Neatly cut a design from one side. Place the cutout piece next to the space. How does it look? You may choose to put it in another place on the puzzle. Continue cutting shapes out of each side of your paper until you have several shapes and no more than half the paper has been cut away.

3. Next, experiment with your puzzle arrangement. When you decide on the best arrangement, carefully glue the pieces on the large sheet of paper.

4. Display your finished puzzle with others from your class.

Art Materials	
Sketch paper	Pencil and eraser
Black, white, and colored construction paper	Glue
	Scissors

THINK SAFETY

Learning Outcomes

1. What is meant by *positive* space and *negative* space?

2. What contrasting colors did you choose for your puzzle? Which shapes look larger, the spaces, or the paper cutout?

3. What is the most interesting part of your puzzle? Explain why you like it.

53 Styles of Printmaking

Observing and Thinking Creatively

Almost 150 years ago, a Japanese man named Utagawa Hiroshige (hir-ə-shē-gā) carved designs into wood blocks, covered them with color, and printed them. He was particularly known for scenes of mist and rain. Look carefully at the **print** shown here. How did Hiroshige create the look of rain?

In this type of print, each color is made by carving a separate block of wood and then covering it with color. How many colors do you see in Hiroshige's print? Hiroshige carved more than fifteen separate blocks to get the result he wanted in some of his prints.

Hiroshige's prints are called **relief prints** because ink is used on the surfaces of the wooden blocks.

In addition to creating prints by carving out areas of wood, prints can be made by building up or cutting apart pieces of cardboard. Some artists cut cardboard shapes like a jigsaw puzzle, ink them with separate colors, put the pieces back together, and make a print. The rubber roller used to spread printing ink is a **brayer**.

In this lesson, you will make a cardboard block and print it two or more times.

Hiroshige, Travellers at Shono in Heavy Rain, woodblock print. Gift of William Sturges Bigelow. Courtesy, Museum of Fine Arts, Boston.

N. Currier, The Road—Winter, 1853, lithograph. Museum of the City of New York.

Instructions for Creating Art

1. Decide what objects you want to include in your design. You may wish to make a geometric shape, leaves, or something that has special meaning to you. Sketch some simple outlines of the shape.

2. Copy your sketch on a piece of thin cardboard or a file folder. Cut out the largest shape. Then draw and cut out any other separate shapes.

3. Glue the largest shape on a rectangular piece of cardboard. Then glue on the smaller pieces. Some pieces may be glued on top of the larger shape. You may wish to glue pieces on top of pieces in many layers.

4. Use a brayer to ink your cardboard block. Then put paper on top of the block and rub the back of the paper. Be sure that you rub the entire area, including the edges. Then remove the paper. This process is called "pulling a print." Many prints can be made from the same block.

Art Materials	
Thin cardboard or a file folder	Brayer
	Pan
Paper	Water-soluble printing ink
Pencil and eraser	
Scissors	Newspaper (to cover work area)
Glue	

THINK SAFETY

Learning Outcomes

1. Describe two ways prints can be made.

2. Describe how you made your cardboard block design and printed it.

3. Of the prints shown here, which design do you like best? Why?

119

54 An Illustrated Alphabet

Observing and Thinking Creatively

How many different kinds of **alphabets** can you name? An alphabet is a set of **symbols** or characters used to represent the sounds of a language. Some alphabet symbols are in a series, like the alphabet used in English, but others are not. In Chinese the characters, called **ideograms**, represent a thing or idea without expressing a particular word for it. Some alphabets have very few symbols, and others, such as the Chinese, have thousands. The alphabet used in the English language is based on one used by the Phoenicians about 3,000 years ago.

Illustrated alphabets are a popular, creative way of teaching letters. Observe the letters shown in this lesson. They were created by Mitsumasa Anno, a popular Japanese illustrator. Each letter appears to be finely crafted from wood. If you look closely, you will notice something strange about each letter in this magical alphabet.

Anno increased the impact of the "V is for violin" idea by making the violin itself in a "v" shape. How many other things can you name that begin with the letter "v"?

In this lesson, you will design a set of alphabet letters with a drawing of an object to illustrate each letter. You will exercise your imagination as you work with lines and shapes in creating your original alphabet.

 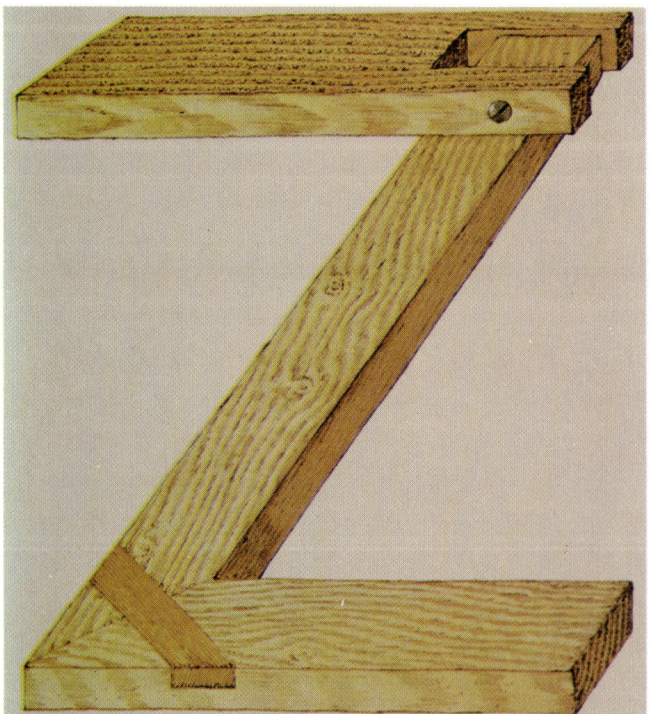

Illustrations of "V", "Z", "M", and "J" from Anno's Alphabet: An Adventure in Imagination by Mitsumasa Anno. Copyright © 1974 by Fukuinkan Shoten. Reprinted by permission of Harper & Row, Publishers, Inc.

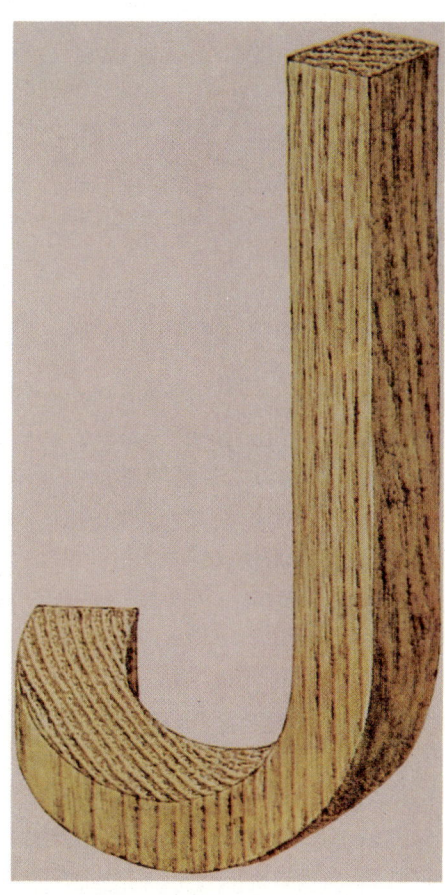

Instructions for Creating Art

1. You may wish to browse through children's alphabet books and magazines for ideas before you begin your own alphabet design. How many different styles of letters can you find? Some artists have developed alphabets around themes such as making each letter look like an animal or object that begins with that letter. Let your imagination be your guide.

2. Practice designing letters on scratch paper until you find a style you like. Work toward making each letter the same size and repeat the lines, curves, and shapes so your set of letters will appear unified.

3. On a piece of drawing paper, draw the first letter and illustration for your alphabet. You may prefer to make all your letters first and then go back to add illustrations. Go over your artwork with colored markers after you have drawn in pencil.

4. When your illustrated alphabet is finished, display it in the classroom. What is the most original idea you included in your alphabet? Is there something in your design that no one else included?

Art Materials

Scratch paper

Drawing paper

Pencil and eraser

Scissors

Colored markers

THINK SAFETY

Learning Outcomes

1. Name two ways alphabets are alike and explain two ways they may be different.

2. Describe what you did to make your illustrated alphabet unique.

3. Describe the theme of your alphabet, and tell why you chose it.

55 Graphic Design with Labels

Observing and Thinking Creatively

Can you think of a sale that is going on somewhere in your town? How did you find out about this sale? You may have heard about it on the radio, but chances are you saw a sign in a window or an advertisement in a newspaper. **Graphic design**, or advertising art, is meant to catch attention and communicate information that will sell a product. How many examples of graphic design can you think of?

Graphic designers work with **color**, **shape**, **composition**, and words. Those who design packages must know which colors catch attention fastest, and which shapes are most attractive to the eye. What are some of the most popular packaging colors? Think about designs that appear on laundry detergents. Which shapes are most repeated? Circles and slanted letters give the idea of action or movement, ideas that fit well with cleaning.

As you walk down a supermarket aisle, which labels catch your eye first? Some label designs are better than others because of color choice and composition. In this lesson, you will design a label. You will increase your awareness of graphic design, shapes, composition, and lettering styles.

Instructions for Creating Art

1. Go on a field trip to a supermarket or look through magazines to study a variety of label designs. Notice what catches your eye as you look around. Choose a product whose label seems dull or one that you think you can improve.

2. Now, examine the product you chose. What are the most attractive features of the product? If it is food, what color is it? Think of a good background for that color. Decide what printing style best captures the mood of the product, and what your own brand name will be.

3. Make practice sketches of label ideas. Experiment with package shape, colors, and lettering for your product. Decide how large the product name will be.

4. Draw your package and label design on a piece of white paper. Carefully letter the words you have chosen for your design. Then paint or color the label.

5. Display your original label design and have classmates tell which parts of the designs they like best.

Art Materials	
Paper	Mixing tray
Pencil and eraser	Container of water
Paints or colored markers	Newspaper (to cover work area)
Brushes	

Learning Outcomes

1. Name three things created by *graphic designers*.

2. Describe how you emphasized the selling features of the product you chose.

3. What do you think is the best improvement in your design? Give reasons for your choice.

56 Greeting Card Designs

Observing and Thinking Creatively

Sending greeting cards is a popular custom in the United States. Billions of cards are produced by several hundred publishers every year. Can you guess which kind of card is the most popular? It is the Christmas card. The first one was designed by John Calcott Horsley in 1843. The card shown here is one of the early Christmas card designs. What features in this card reveal that it was designed many years ago?

Greeting cards have been made of paper, cardboard, cloth, leather, and even glass. They can be small, large, square, rectangular, or circular. Artists who create greeting card designs are **graphic designers**. How many different occasions for greeting cards can you name? Did you remember Halloween and "bon voyage" cards?

Although there are many greeting cards available, sometimes it is difficult to find one that looks just right and says exactly what you want. Designing and making your own greeting card will be fun for you, and the card will also please the person who receives it.

In this lesson, you will design and make a greeting card for someone special. You increase your awareness of careful **lettering** and you will experiment with **composition** and **details** to make your greeting card pleasing in its design and message.

Instructions for Creating Art

1. Decide on the type of card you will make. Then choose the person you want to receive your handmade, individually designed card. Think about the people, places, and things this person likes. Use these ideas to help you design the card.

2. Next, choose the color of construction paper you want your card to be. Decide on the size and shape of your card, and cut it out. Fold the shape in half.

3. On a separate piece of paper, practice writing a message. You may wish to make up a poem or rhyme for the person. You might write something funny or something serious. Whatever you choose, practice printing the message clearly with the letters evenly spaced. Be sure your message will fit neatly on the card.

4. When you have a neat, clear copy of the message you wish to use, carefully letter it on a piece of paper and cut it out.

5. On another piece of paper, illustrate your message. You might make a collage of magazine pictures of things that interest the person who will receive your card. You might create an **abstract** design from a variety of colored papers. Experiment until the arrangement of your message and your illustration pleases you. Then glue them to the card you cut out. Give your card at the appropriate time.

Art Materials

Construction paper in different colors	Colored markers
	Glue
Scissors	Ribbons, photos, magazines, sequins, etc.
White paper	
Pencil and eraser	

Learning Outcomes

1. What aspects of art are used in making a greeting card?

2. Describe how you made your illustration and design especially suit the person you chose.

3. What is your favorite occasion to receive greeting cards? Why?

57 Poem Illustrations

Observing and Thinking Creatively

The poems and illustrations shown here are the work of two very popular writers who also **illustrate** their own work. Arnold Lobel may be best known for his Frog and Toad series. He was raised by grandparents in New York, and says he was a lonely, rather unhappy child whose favorite activity was watching "Kukla, Fran, and Ollie" on TV. His wife Anita is also an artist. Lobel has the ability to create comic characters with just a few simple lines and pictures. What makes this poem and illustration seem humorous?

Shel Silverstein's poetry anthologies *Where the Sidewalk Ends* and *A Light in the Attic* include very unusual, humorous subjects. He writes about a girl who will not take the garbage out, a boy who has a hot dog for a pet, a dentist who disappears while working on an alligator's teeth, and other whimsical topics. What is funny about the "Anteater" shown here? Silverstein's line drawings are done in black and white.

Both Lobel and Silverstein are **illustrators**. They provide pictures and details that help the reader understand and visualize characters in their poem stories.

In this lesson, you will write and illustrate some humorous poems of your own.

Although he didn't like the taste,
George brushed his teeth with pickle paste.
Not ever was his mouth so clean,
Not ever were his teeth so green.

Arnold Lobel, "George the Cat" (with Poem). Reprinted from Whiskers and Rhymes *by Arnold Lobel, Copyright © 1985 by Arnold Lobel, used by permission of Greenwillow Books, New York.*

ANTEATER

"A genuine anteater,"
The pet man told my dad.
Turned out, it was an *aunt* eater,
And now my uncle's mad!

"Anteater" from A LIGHT IN THE ATTIC: Poems and Drawings by Shel Silverstein. Copyright © 1981 by Snake Eye Music, Inc. Reproduced by permission of Harper and Row, Publishers, Inc.

Instructions for Creating Art

1. Think of a subject for your poem. You might write about a brother or sister, a pet, or you may make up a character. Your poem may be a simple four-line rhyme, like those in the lesson, or it may be longer. Write two or three poems.

2. Now decide how you will illustrate your poems. What features will you emphasize on your characters? Arnold Lobel drew three colored pictures to illustrate his poem about pickle toothpaste, but Shel Silverstein did a single line drawing. Which style fits the poems you have written? Make practice sketches of your illustrations before you do the final ones.

3. Carefully print each poem on a separate sheet of white paper. Then draw your illustrations. Color them if you wish.

4. When you have completed your poem illustrations, **bind** them into a book with others from your class.

Art Materials	
Colored markers or pencils, oil pastels, crayons, or chalk	Drawing paper Pencil and eraser

Learning Outcomes

1. What does an *illustrator* do?

2. Describe how you illustrated the poems you wrote.

3. Choose the poem illustration from the lesson you like best, and tell what you like about it.

58 Technical Drawing and Process Illustration

Observing and Thinking Creatively

Can you name an example of **mechanical drawing**? This form of art is used by architects and engineers. Using mechanical devices such as a **compass** and **T square**, a **draftsman** makes detailed, accurate, precise drawings so someone can construct a design. Computers, telephones, lamps, and automobiles must first exist as mechanical drawings before they can be built. Precise, exact drawing that is done without mechanical measuring instruments is called **technical drawing** or sketching.

Another type of **illustration** gives information to reinforce the meaning of the **text**, or words. Illustrations can be found in science books, how-to-do-it books, cookbooks, and similar sources. They appear with instructions on how to assemble models, bicycles, vacuum cleaners, furniture, toys, and so on.

Illustrations are often used to explain a process. Look at the examples in this lesson. Notice how simple outlines are used and only necessary details are shown. In this lesson, you will illustrate a process.

1. Pick Leaves.
2. Press them in a book for 2 hours to make them flat. Then remove.
3. Dab paint on leaves with sponge.
4. Arrange on a piece of paper.
5. Cover with paper towel and roll.
6. Let dry.

Loosen the nuts.

Lift up the car.

Take off the nuts.

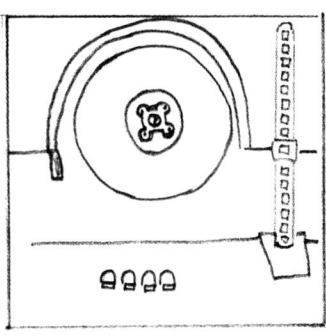
Change the tire.

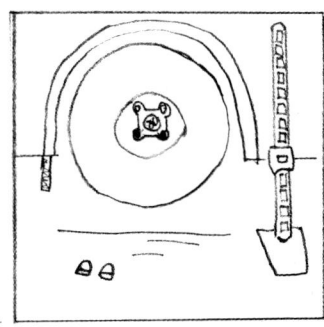
Replace the nuts.

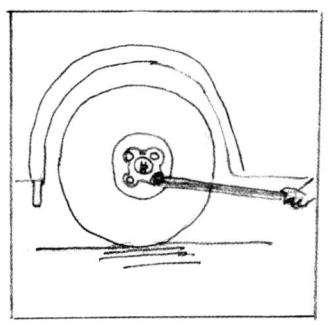
Lower the car and tighten the nuts.

Instructions for Creating Art

1. First, think of a process you understand well. It should have between four and eight steps. What do you know how to do that you might explain to someone else? Perhaps you could illustrate the process of bathing a pet, making a model, or building a project. You might illustrate emergency procedures for an earthquake or tornado, what to do for an injury, or how to prepare a certain food.

2. Make practice sketches of your idea. Your process should be simple and should not require a great amount of text. Write the words that explain your process. They must be simple and printed small enough to fit the frames for your process. Using a ruler, draw one frame for each step.

3. Now, using a black felt-tip pen and a ruler, draw your finished process in frames. Add the text. You may wish to color or **highlight** important parts in the process.

4. Label your process and display it with others from your class. As you look at other processes, is there enough information for you to do the process? Can students follow the directions for your process?

Art Materials	
Paper	Black felt-tip pen
Pencil and eraser	Ruler
Colored markers	

Learning Outcomes

1. Describe two tasks which require *mechanical drawing*.

2. Describe how you illustrated a process. Which parts did you highlight?

3. Would you be interested in a career that uses mechanical drawing or illustration? Why or why not?

59 Cartoon Art

Observing and Thinking Creatively

When something funny or good happens in your life, what is one of the first things you want to do? Most of us want to share our experiences with others. **Cartoon** art is a special way of communicating ideas and feelings with others.

A series of related cartoons that tell a story is called a **comic strip**. The first comic strip to achieve popularity was "Hogan's Alley." This comic strip appeared in the Sunday edition of *New York World* in 1895. Since that time, Sunday "funnies" have become a standard part of American life.

Comic strip stories deal with detectives, super heroes, animals, cavemen, and Army life. Some series contain humorous comments about social and political happenings. Can you name characters from each of these types of comics? What other types of comics can you identify? Comic strips lost some of their popularity after television became widespread. Why do you think this happened?

Because of the very limited space available for comics, a **cartoonist** must plan his or her story very carefully. Characters must be simple and easy to recognize. Stories must fit into four or five frames, so they cannot be complicated.

In this lesson, you will make up a simple story with original characters to illustrate your own comic strip.

Charles Schulz, Peanuts, copyright © 1962 United Feature Syndicate, Inc.

Instructions for Creating Art

1. You may wish to look through comic strips in comic books or newspapers for ideas before you begin.

2. Think of a humorous incident you observed or experienced. Is there something funny about your morning routine in getting ready for school? Perhaps you've laughed at events that occur when people are late. Think of the idea you will use for your story and decide how many characters you will use. Remember, your story will have to fit in four or five frames, so it must be simple.

3. Lightly sketch your idea. Make the characters simple and exaggerate some of their characteristics. *Note:* It is illegal to use cartoon characters you have seen before. These designs belong to their creators.

4. Draw a series of four to five frames. Sketch your ideas in each frame, leaving room for the words you want to add. Then go over your drawings with colored markers or crayons. Use a black felt-tip pen to write the words in the frames.

5. Give your comic strip a name and display it with others in your classroom.

Art Materials

White paper	Pencil and eraser
Colored markers or crayons	Black felt-tip pen

Learning Outcomes

1. What is the difference between a comic strip and a story in your language or reading book?

2. Describe the characters you created for your comic strip. What characteristics did you exaggerate? How did you exaggerate those characteristics?

3. Name your favorite cartoon character, and tell what you like about that particular character.

60 Art on Film

Observing and Thinking Creatively

Until 1889, artists were able to show **space**, time, and motion only with swirling lines or repeated figures on paper or canvas. But in 1889, Thomas Edison invented a camera that could take pictures one immediately after another, giving the **illusion** of motion. The first fifteen-minute movie was shown in Paris in 1895, and a new art form began.

Motion pictures now explore many kinds of space—outer space, underwater, and the inner space of feelings and thoughts. Making a film requires teamwork among a scriptwriter, director, cameramen, sound men, musicians, actors, set and costume designers, editors, and makeup designers.

Camera techniques have changed greatly since the beginning of motion pictures. In the first movies, the camera showed a whole scene and very little movement. Now lenses zoom in close and even the simple action of shifting eyes or a nodding head is caught.

The first motion picture stories were silent, so stories were told with gestures. If you can, see an old Charlie Chaplin film and observe how he communicates through movement and expression. The first American "talkie" was *The Jazz Singer*, released in 1927.

Each scene of a movie must be planned. The best angle must be chosen, and the **composition** or arrangement of the scene must be carefully balanced. Before a scene is shot, it is first sketched on a **storyboard**. Each scene is drawn in miniature with a description of what is happening. In this way a director can see how the finished picture will appear.

In this lesson, you will create a storyboard and make your own filmstrip.

© Lucasfilm Ltd. (LFL) 1983. All rights reserved.

© Lucasfilm Ltd. (LFL) 1983. All rights reserved.

Instructions for Creating Art

1. Think of a story you want to tell. You may wish to illustrate a short story, fairy tale, or play, or you may create an original story. You might also illustrate a historical event or focus on your family, town, school, or pet. You might create a filmstrip about how to do something. Decide on a theme or story, and then write a list of 10 to 20 **scenes**, or episodes, that illustrate it.

2. Prepare a **storyboard** with a sketch of each scene and a brief description of what is happening. Decide how many frames you will fill with your story. See the storyboard illustrations in this lesson.

3. Allow six inches of blank film before you make your first drawing. The film should be unrolled up and down on your desk, with pictures being drawn between the side holes. Place a 1" by 1¼" paper rectangle on the film where your first drawing will be and make some light marks on each outside edge in the area where the holes are.

4. Using a felt-tip pen, draw the first scene on your list directly on the film between the marks you made. Then use colored pens to fill in the shapes in your picture.

5. Next, mark off another square directly below the first drawing. Make your second drawing in this square. Continue in this manner until all the frames of your story are completed.

6. When your filmstrip pictures are dry, project them on the screen and narrate your story for the class.

Art Materials

Paper and pencil	1" × 1¼" paper rectangle
35mm blank film	
Fine colored felt-tip markers	Film projector and screen

Learning Outcomes

1. Explain how a *storyboard* is used.

2. Describe the characters you created for your film, and tell how you communicated their personalities or other features.

3. Which is the best illustrated segment of your filmstrip? Why do you think so?

Exploring Art

Showing Art

Art provides a sense of pleasure and enjoyment for both the artist who creates it and those who view it. Where can you go to see art? Schools often have art shows during the year to display artwork from a single class or the entire school. District art shows that feature work from several schools are sometimes held in the spring.

Works of art may also be seen in a **gallery** or **museum** of art. A gallery is a room or building used only for displaying artwork. An art museum is an institution that acquires, displays, and cares for paintings, sculpture, and other artwork. Museums also provide other special services, such as lectures, guided tours, concerts, and sometimes art classes. Some museums have special collections of one type of artwork, such as the Museum of Navajo Ceremonial Arts in Santa Fe, New Mexico. This museum features sand paintings and other forms of art used in Navajo rituals.

Careers associated with museums include the positions of **registrar**, **curator**, **conservator**, **designer**, **preparator**, and **guard**. The registrar records a description of each art object, has it photographed, and gives it a number. A curator researches each object and decides how it is to be displayed. The conservators clean, preserve, or restore the art objects before they are displayed. Designers build display cases, and preparators create display backgrounds and prepare written information about the exhibit. Museum guards patrol the exhibits to protect them from loss or harm. Many museums have elaborate security systems.

For this activity, you will participate with your class in organizing an art show. Prepare items and display them attractively. Include the title and artist of each artwork. Decide which items you will group together, and how many pieces each student may submit. Invite your schoolmates to attend your art show.

Review

Using What You Have Learned

Do you recognize the objects in these photographs? They are commonly found on streets, and the tops lift off. Another type of round art, these objects are manhole covers. Although they are ordinary objects that usually go unnoticed, manhole covers carry designs and communicate ideas. Examine the examples shown here and see how many artistic elements you can identify from your study of design.

1. Identify any examples of the **universal symbols**. Which of the manhole designs includes more symbols? Identify as many symbols as you can.
2. Are these manholes examples of **symmetrical** or **asymmetrical balance**? How can you tell?
3. Which design looks most **unified**? Why do you think so?
4. Which manhole shows the best example of **pattern**? What makes you say so? What basic **shapes** are repeated most in each manhole?
5. Which manhole shows the most creative use of **line**? Explain the reasons for your choice. Identify the **center of interest** of each manhole.
6. Tell which design you prefer, and why.

135

Glossary

abstract A style that uses shapes, designs, textures, and colors to depict an object in a way that may not look real but that emphasizes moods or feelings. Abstract art often uses geometrical shapes and bold, bright colors.

accuracy Correctness or exactness.

alphabet A set of symbols or characters used to represent the sounds of a language.

analogous colors Colors that are closely related. For example, blue, blue-violet, and violet all have the color blue in common. Families of analogous colors include the warm colors (red, orange, and yellow) and the cool colors (blue, green, and violet).

appliqué A design made by stitching pieces of colored fabric onto a larger piece of cloth. Appliqué is used for wall hangings and as decoration on clothing, quilts, and pillows.

archaeologists People who learn about past civilizations by digging up and studying the remains of their cultures, including tools, weapons, and pottery.

architect A person who designs and draws plans for buildings.

architecture The art of designing and constructing buildings.

association The act of linking an image in thought or memory with a person or thing. What idea do you associate with a particular sound, such as a cricket chirping?

asymmetrical /ā′-sə-me′-tri-kəl/ Having a kind of balance in which the two sides of an artwork are not exactly alike, but still look balanced.

background Parts of an artwork that are in the distance. The background is located behind the foreground and middle ground.

balance The arrangement of the parts of an artwork, including color, sizes, and numbers of objects, to achieve a sense of equality. Balance may be symmetrical, asymmetrical, or radial. Balance is a principle of design.

banner A flag or other piece of cloth that may have a sign, name, or slogan written on it. Banners often come before a marching band.

bark cloth A cloth made by taking the white inner fibers from tree bark and beating them together into a fine cloth. May be called *tapa*.

bas-relief /bä′-ri-lēf/ A French word meaning "low-raised work." This art is also called *relief sculpture*.

bind To fasten together.

blind contour drawing A kind of drawing done in one continuous line, in which the pencil is kept moving while the eyes remain on the object, never looking down at the paper. (*See also* contour drawing.)

brayer /brā′-er/ A small roller used to spread printing ink evenly on a surface before printing.

calligraphy /kə-lig′-rə-fē/ The art of writing letters and words in an ornamental style using brushes or pens.

cartoon A kind of drawing done to make people laugh or to entertain them with adventure. A cartoon usually has simple lines, uses basic colors, and tells a story in one picture or a series of pictures called *frames*.

cartoonist An artist who draws cartoons or comic strips for newspapers, magazines, motion pictures, and so on.

center The middle point of anything. The center is the same distance from opposite edges.

center of interest The most important part in a work of art. All the other parts should center around, provide background for, or draw attention to the center of interest.

circle A round, two-dimensional shape in which every point on the outside line is the same distance from the center.

closed shape Space that is completely enclosed by a line. For example, a triangle is a closed shape. (*See also* open shape and empty shape.)

coils Long, snake-like strips of clay that are used in making pottery.

collage /kə-läzh′/ A work of art created by gluing bits of paper, fabric, scraps, photographs, or other materials to a flat surface.

color The hue, value, and intensity of an object. The *primary colors* are red, yellow, and blue; every color except white can be created by combining these three colors. Color is an element of design.

color scheme The colors an artist uses and the way they are combined in an artwork.

column A slender, round, upright pillar or post. Often used to support part of a building.

comic strip A group of simple drawings that tells a story or part of a story.

compass A mechanical tool that has two hinged, adjustable legs for drawing different sizes of circles and arcs. One of the legs has a sharp steel point that is placed on one spot on the paper. The other end holds a pencil that rotates around the pointed end, making a circle.

complementary colors Colors that are opposites on the color wheel and contrast with each other. For example, orange is the complement of blue, violet is the complement of yellow, and so on. When two complementary colors are mixed together, they make the neutral colors of brown or gray.

compose To create, put together, or arrange.

composition The arrangement of shapes and colors of a painting or sculpture. The composition of a work should be pleasing, decorative or expressive, and well-designed. The term also refers to any work of art.

contour The outline or edge of a figure or object. In contour drawing, a single line is used to draw the outline of an object.

contour drawing A drawing of an object using one continuous line to show the outer and inner outlines of an object.

contrast A large difference between two things; for example, hot and cold, yellow and purple, and light and shadow. Contrasting values, colors, and textures add excitement, emphasis, and interest to an artwork.

cool colors The family of related colors ranging from the greens through the blues and violets. (*See also* analogous colors)

costume Clothing characteristic of a particular time, place, or people.

Cubism A style of art developed primarily by Pablo Piscasso. In this art style, the subject is viewed from all sides, then broken apart and reassembled in an abstract form to show all these parts at once, emphasizing geometric shapes.

cutout In art, a piece of paper cut into a shape and arranged with other cutouts to form designs and pictures.

depth The apparent distance from front to back or near to far in an artwork. Techniques of *perspective* are used to create the illusion of depth in paintings and drawings.

design An organized and creative arrangement made of patterns, lines, textures, shapes, colors, and so on.

detail A distinctive feature of an object or scene which can be seen most clearly close up. Also, a small part of a work of art, enlarged to show a close-up of its features.

distort To change the way something looks to make it more interesting or meaningful, usually by twisting it out of its proper or natural form or by exaggerating some of its features.

distorting The process used to distort something.

dome A round roof shaped like half a ball, supported by a circular or many-sided base.

dominant The part of a design that is the most important, powerful, or has the most influence. A certain color can be dominant, and so can an object, line, shape, or texture.

Doric architecture A style of Greek architecture characterized by large, fluted columns.

draftsman An artist who draws plans and sketches of machinery and buildings.

earth colors Colors found naturally in the environment, including brown, brownish-yellow, and brownish-red.

elements of design Basic parts which are put together to compose an artwork. These include line, shape, space, texture, color, and value.

emboss To create a raised design or relief on a flat surface by pressing or hammering a design into the back side.

emphasis The use of opposing sizes or shapes, contrasting colors, or other means to draw attention to certain areas or objects in a work of art. Emphasis is a principle of design.

empty shape In an artwork, a shape that is left bare instead of filled with lines or color.

exterior Something that is outside. For example, an *exterior* wall is on the outside of a building.

fiber art Art using thread, yarn, or fabric, such as weaving.

filmstrip A strip of film bearing a series of pictures for one-by-one projection on a screen.

fire To bake shaped clay in a kiln to make hard pottery.

fixative A thin liquid that is sprayed over pastels and drawings to keep them from smearing or rubbing off the paper.

fluted Having rounded grooves or channels.

foil relief An artwork made by rubbing a piece of foil over a built up or textured surface to create a raised design on the foil.

foreground The part of a work of art that appears to be in front, nearest to the viewer. Usually, the objects that are on the lower part of a picture appear to be in the foreground.

form An object that has depth as well as height and width. For example, a triangle, which is two-dimensional, is a *shape,* but a pyramid, which is three-dimensional, is a *form.* Also, a style of creating art according to a certain standard or technique.

frame A boxed-in picture in a series of pictures, such as a comic strip, filmstrip, or set of illustrations.

frieze Decorative relief of figures carved in a horizontal band around a building. Popular in Greek architecture.

galleries Rooms where paintings or other artworks are displayed and sold.

geometric Refers to simple shapes such as triangles, squares, and circles.

gradated wash A wash that is light at the top, where little color has been applied, and that gradually becomes darker at the bottom, where more color has been applied.

gradation /grā-dā′′-shən/ A gradual, smooth change from light to dark, rough to smooth, or one color to another.

graphic design Art for commercial purposes, including packages, advertisements, signs, books and magazines, and pamphlets.

graphic designer A person who designs art for commercial purposes, such as for packages, advertisements, signs, books, and magazines.

greeting card A card with a message, usually sent or given on a special occasion, such as a birthday or holiday.

hand puppet A small, hollow cloth figure, usually of a person or animal, that fits over and is moved by the hand.

harmonious colors Colors that look well together because they are complementary, analogous, or otherwise related.

highlight To center attention on or emphasize through use of color.

highlighting The process of emphasizing through use of color.

high relief In *relief sculpture,* a form that extends at least halfway out of the background. (*See also* middle relief, low relief.)

horizon A level line where water or land seems to end and the sky begins.

horizontal Straight and flat across, parallel to the horizon. A *horizontal* painting is wider than it is tall.

ideogram A picture or symbol used in a writing system that represents a thing or idea instead of a letter or specific word, as in Chinese writing.

illusion A deceptive or misleading image or idea.

illustrate To create designs and pictures for books or magazines to make clear or explain the text or show what happens in a story.

illustration A design or picture in a book or magazine that explains the text or shows what happens in the story.

illustrator A person who creates designs and pictures for books and magazines.

image A mental picture, idea, or impression of a person, thing, or idea that can be represented visually.

Impressionism An art movement which concentrated on showing the effects of light on things at different times of day. Impressionists use unblended dots and slashes of pure color placed close together to create a mood or *impression* of a scene.

intensity The brightness or dullness of a hue or color. For example, the intensity of the pure color blue is very bright. When a lighter or darker color is added to blue, the intensity is less bright, or subdued.

kiln /kil or kiln/ A special oven or furnace that can reach very high temperatures and is used to bake, or *fire,* clay.

kinetic /kə-net′-ik/ Expressing motion. In art, kinetic refers to sculpture that moves, such as a *mobile* or *stabile.*

landscape A scene or view on land, such as mountains, rivers, flowers, fields, or forests.

lettering Drawing or creating letters used in a word or saying.

line The outline or contour of an object. Line can be two-dimensional, three-dimensional, or implied. Line is an element of design.

linear perspective Showing depth and distance in a picture by making lines that are parallel in nature get closer together in the distance of an artwork, and by making objects smaller in the distance than in the foreground.

line drawing A picture composed only of lines, having no shading or color.

lithograph A type of printing invented in 1798, in which a picture or design is drawn on a smooth stone with a special crayon. The stone is then treated with a chemical that allows the ink to stick only where the crayon was used. Finally, the surface is inked and the crayon design is printed on paper.

low relief In relief sculpture, a very slight extension of a form out of the background. (*See also* high relief and middle relief.)

marionette /mar-ē-ə-net′/ A small, complete figure, usually of a person or animal and made of wood, that is moved from above by strings that are attached to its jointed arms, legs, and body.

mass The area inside a shape.

mechanical drawing Drawing done with the help of mechanical tools or instruments, such as a compass and a T square.

medal A flat piece of metal that is embossed or engraved with a design and given to honor or remember a person or event. A medal is often coin-shaped.

medallion A large medal usually worn around the neck on a heavy chain, ribbon, or rope.

medium In art, the material an artist uses—oil, watercolor, pen and ink, chalk, and so on. (The plural form is *media.*)

middle ground The part of a work of art that lies between the foreground and the background.

middle relief In relief sculpture, a form that extends about one-quarter of the way out of the background. (*See also* high relief, low relief.)

mobile /mō′-bēl/ A type of sculpture in which objects are hung and balanced so that they are moved by currents of air. The mobile as an art form was introduced by Alexander Calder in the 1930's.

model A person who poses for an artist. Also, a small-sized copy of something. For example, architects make small models of buildings with furnishings and landscaping to show clients how the finished product will look.

molas /mō′-läz/ Appliqué designs made by the Cuna Indians in which several layers of cloth are sewn together and the top layers are cut and turned to show the colors underneath.

monochrome Having only a single color; may include its *tints* and *shades.*

monument A building, statue, or other structure especially built to remember and honor a person or event.

mood An overall feeling or emotion.

mosaic /mō-zā′-ik/ A picture or design made by fitting into plaster or cement tiny pieces of colored paper, glass, tile, stone, or other similar materials.

movement The arrangement of the parts of a design to create a sense of motion by using lines that cause the eye to move over the work. Also, a tendency or trend by artists during a period to use certain techniques or methods.

mural A very large painting that covers a wall. It can be painted right on the wall, or on paper, canvas, or wood to be attached to the wall.

museum A building where objects of interest or value are collected and displayed.

negative space Empty space in an artwork. (*See also* positive space.)

neutral A color not associated with a hue. Neutral colors include black, white, gray, and brown. A hue can be *neutralized* by adding some of its complement to it.

non-objective Without a recognizable object.

one point perspective A form of *linear perspective* in which all lines appear to meet at a single point on the horizon.

oblong A shape stretched out from a circle or square shape so that it is longer than it is wide.

opaque /ō-pāk′/ Something that cannot be seen through; the opposite of transparent.

open shape Space that is not completely enclosed by a line. For example, a square with all or part of one side missing is an open shape. (*See also* closed shape.)

optical mixing The blending by the eyes of pure colors placed next to each other in a work of art. For example, if dots of yellow are placed next to dots of blue, the colors will appear to merge into a bright green color when viewed from a distance. Optical mixing is important in Impressionistic painting.

oval An egg-like shape that looks like a circle that has been stretched to make it longer. The two ends of an oval may or may not be the same size and shape.

overlap To extend over or rest on top of something and partly cover it up.

pattern The repetition of shapes, lines, or colors in a design. A pattern can also be a model or mold designed to be copied.

pendant An ornamental piece worn around the neck on a light chain or ribbon.

perception The process of becoming aware through sight, sound, taste, smell, or touch.

photographic Showing people and objects with the exactness of color, shape, and detail as they would appear in a photograph.

pigment Coloring matter, usually a powder, that mixes with water, oil, or other substances to make colored paints and dyes.

plane Any flat surface.

pointillism A method of painting developed in France in the 1880's in which tiny dots of color are applied to a canvas. When viewed from a distance, the points of color appear to blend together to make other colors and to form shapes and outlines. (*See also* optical mixing.)

portrait A painting, sculpture, drawing, photo, or other work of art showing a person, several people, or an animal. Portraits usually show only the face, but can include part or all of the body as well.

positive space Space in an artwork that is filled with something, such as lines, designs, color, or shapes. (*See also* negative space.)

power loom A machine that weaves threads or yarn into fabric.

pre-Columbian Belonging to the time before the arrival of Columbus in the Americas.

press print A print made by pressing an inked object onto paper to transfer a design.

primary colors The hues red, yellow, and blue, which in different combinations produce all other colors except white. The primary colors cannot be produced by mixing any other colors.

primitive Early or undeveloped; simple.

principles of design Guidelines that aid in arranging and composing attractive designs. These include balance, contrast, variety, pattern, rhythm, emphasis, and unity.

print A shape or mark made from a printing block or other object that is covered with wet color and then pressed on a flat surface, such as paper or cloth. Most prints can be repeated over and over again by re-inking the printing block. Prints can be made in many ways, including using an engraved block or stone, transfer paper, or a film negative.

profile An outline of an object, usually a drawing or painting of the side view of a person's face

proportion The relationship of the size of one part to another or to the whole. In painting and sculpture, for example, an artist tries to achieve the right relationship in size or *proportion* of a nose to a head, and a head to a body.

pyramid A solid, three-dimensional shape that is square at the bottom and has four triangle-shaped sides that meet in a point at the top.

radial balance A type of balance based on a circle with lines extending from a central point. A wheel with spokes is an example of radial balance.

realism A style of art in which artists try to show objects, scenes, and people as they actually appear.

realistic Looking like real people, objects, or places as we actually see them. Realistic art portrays lifelike colors, textures, shadows, proportions, and so on.

rectangle A two-dimensional shape with four sides and four right angles. The top and bottom may be longer or shorter than the sides, or they may be equal, as in a square.

reflection An image given back by a reflecting surface, such as a mirror or a still lake.

relief print A print made by a printing block with raised designs, which are inked and pressed onto a surface.

relief sculpture An artwork in which forms rise up from a flat or hollowed out background.

Renaissance /ren'-ə-säns/ A period that began in Italy after the Middle Ages and lasted from about A.D. 1400 to 1600. The period was characterized by a renewed interest in ancient Greek and Roman design and included an emphasis on human beings, their environment, science, and philosophy.

representation Having objects and people you can recognize, as opposed to *abstract*.

reverse appliqué A design made by stitching several layers of cloth together, then cutting away and turning under some of the top layers to show the colors underneath. (*See also* appliqué.)

rhythm Regular repetition of lines, shapes, colors, or patterns in a work of art.

rod puppet A small, movable figure of a person or animal that is controlled by rods or sticks inserted from below. Rod puppets are popular in Japan, China, and Russia.

rule of compensation A guideline for balancing a composition that states that the bigger the mass, the more toward the center of an artwork it should be placed. Similarly, the smaller the mass, the more toward the edge it is placed.

scoring To make scratches and creases in pieces of clay to be joined together. Scoring and applying slip to the roughened surfaces creates a bond that holds the pieces together.

seascape A picture of a scene at sea or a scene including a portion of the sea.

shade A color to which black or another dark hue has been added to make it darker. For example, black added to red produces a darker *shade* of red. (*See also* tint.)

shading Showing gradual change from light to dark or dark to light in a picture by darkening areas that would be shadowed and leaving other areas light. Shading is used to create the illusions of *dimension* and *depth*.

shape A two-dimensional figure outlined by lines or a change in color or shading. A triangle is a shape. Shape is an element of design. (*See also* form.)

silhouette /sil-ə-wet'/ A dark outline of a solid shape without any details, like a shadow.

slip A creamy mixture of clay and water used to cement two pieces of clay together, such as a handle and a cup. Slip can also be used for dripping on pottery as decoration.

space The distance, area, or depth shown in a work of art. Also the open parts between or inside shapes. Space is an element of design.

split complements One color plus the two colors that are on either side of its complement on the color wheel. For example, the complement of blue is orange, and the two colors on either side of orange are yellow-orange and red-orange. Therefore, the split complements of blue are yellow-orange and red-orange.

square A two-dimensional shape with four equal sides and four equal angles.

stabile /stā′-bēl/ An abstract sculpture that has movable parts similar to a *mobile,* but that is attached to a solid, unmovable base rather than suspended.

still life A drawing or painting of an arrangement of nonmoving, nonliving objects, such as fruit, flowers, or bottles. Usually, a still life is set indoors and contains at least one man-made object, such as a vase or bowl.

Stone Age The first known period of prehistoric human culture, during which work was done with stone tools.

storyboard A series of simple pictures that depict the important changes of scene and action in a planned filmstrip, movie, or television show.

style An artist's particular way of expressing, using materials, constructing, or designing that is characteristic of a person, group, or culture.

subdue To make less intense.

Surrealism A style of painting that emphasizes images from the unconscious mind, such as from dreams or fantasies. Surrealistic artists make unusual or impossible combinations of things and paint them in a realistic way.

symbol Something that stands for something else, especially a letter, figure, or sign that represents a real object or idea.

symmetrical /sə-me′-tri-kəl/ Having a kind of balance in which things on each side of a center line are identical. For example, the two halves of a person's face are symmetrical.

tapa A coarse cloth made from pounded bark and decorated with geometric designs.

technical drawing Precise, exact drawing that is done without mechanical measuring instruments.

tempera An opaque, water-soluble paint available in liquid or powder form also called poster paint.

tesserae /tes′-ə-rē/ The individual pieces used in making a mosaic.

text The main body of words in a book, magazine, pamphlet, or other printed work.

texture The way a surface looks and feels—rough, smooth, silky, and so on.

three-dimensional Having length, width, and depth. A sculpture is three-dimensional, but a drawing is two-dimensional because it is flat and has only length and width, not depth.

tint A color to which white has been added. For example, white added to blue makes a lighter blue *tint.* (*See also* shade.)

tone The tint, shade, brightness, or value of a color.

topography A description, drawing, or model of mountains, valleys, hills, rivers, roads, bridges, and other things found on the surface of a place.

tower A tall, vertical structure that either stands free or is part of a building.

transformation A change in shape or appearance.

transparent Allowing light to pass through so that objects can be clearly seen underneath; the opposite of opaque. Window glass, cellophane, and watercolors are *transparent.*

triad Three colors equally spaced on the color wheel. For example, yellow, blue, and red form a *triad,* as do green, purple, and orange, and so on.

triangle A figure with three sides and three angles.

T square A long, flat ruler that is attached to a short piece that makes it look like a "T". The short piece slides along the edge of a drawing board to position the ruler so parallel lines can be drawn.

turret A small tower, usually containing stairs, that is located on the top of a building.

two-dimensional Having height and width, such as a drawing. A sculpture, which has depth in addition to height and width, is *three-dimensional.*

unity The appearance of oneness or wholeness achieved when all parts of an artwork look as though they belong together. This sense of harmony occurs when the parts are balanced, are related to each other, and produce a desired effort.

universal symbols Seven symbols found in patterns created all over the world. To see these symbols, turn to page 75.

value The lightness or darkness of tones or colors. For example, white and yellow have a light value and black and purple have a dark value. Value is an element of design.

value scale A series of spaces filled with the tints and shades of one color, starting with the lightest tint on one end, and gradually changing into the darkest shade on the other.

vanishing point In linear perspective, the place on the horizon where parallel lines seem to meet.

variety Different types or an assortment of lines, shapes, or textures in a work of art. Variety is a principle of design.

vertical Going straight up and down. A *vertical* painting is taller than it is wide.

vexillographers Those who design and make flags.

viewfinder A small window cut in a piece of paper that shows what will be in a picture.

visualize To see or form a mental picture of something.

warm colors The family of related colors ranging from the reds through the oranges and yellows. (*See also* analogous colors.)

warp The vertical threads that are attached to the top and bottom of a loom, through which the weft is woven. (*See also* weft.)

wash The background of a watercolor picture, prepared using thin, watery paint applied quickly with large, sweeping brushstrokes.

watercolor A transparent paint made by mixing powdered colors with a binding agent and water. The term also refers to a painting done with watercolors.

waterscape A painting of or including a body of water.

weaving The interlacing of yarn or thread to make cloth.

weft The threads or strands of yarn that are woven over and under the warp threads to make a solid weaving. (*See also* warp.)

Artists' Reference

All the works by famous artists presented in this book are listed here. Use this list to locate particular paintings, drawings, sculptures, and other artworks and to find works by artists who especially interest you.

Adams, Herbert — *Singing Boys* 84
Allen, Jesse — *The Banyon Tree* 24
Allston, Washington — *Belshazzar's Left Hand* 8
Anno, Mitsumasa — *Anno's Alphabet* 120, 121
Boccioni, Umberto — *The City Rises* 39
Calder, Alexander — *Untitled (Mobile)* 30
Fish Mobile 1
Drawing for *Aesop's Fables* (Camel) 4
Cohoon, Hannah — *The Tree of Light* or *Blazing Tree* 25
Currier, Nathaniel — *The Road—Winter* 119
Dali, Salvador — *The Persistence of Memory* 114
da Vinci, Leonardo — *Mona Lisa* 50
Degas, Edgar — *Ballerina* 82
Delaunay, Robert — *Political Drama* 23
Dufy, Raoul — *Le Haras du Pin* 33
Dürer, Albrecht — *Rhinoceros* 2
Young Woman in Netherlandish Dress 51
Eakins, Thomas — *Max Schmidt in a Single Scull* 56
El Greco — *View of Toledo* 49
Escher, M. C. — *Drawing Hands* 112
Sky and Water I 110
Relativity 113
Freeman, Nancy — *The Fish Market* 70
Gainsborough, Thomas — *Landscape with a Bridge* 10
Gauguin, Paul — *Woman with Mango* 38
Gericault, Theodore — *Horse Race at the Start* 35
Grandeville — *Heads of Men and Animals Compared* 110
Harnett, William — *My Gems* 57
Hassam, Childe — *Boston Commons at Twilight* 90
Hiroshige — *Travelers at Shono in Heavy Rain* 118
Hokusai — *Tuning the Samisen* 27

Holbein III, Hans	*Henry VIII* 54
Holmquist, Anders	*Wings* 104
Homer, Winslow	*Mink Pond* 46
	Snap the Whip 57
Hurd, Peter	*Eve of St. John* 48
Landseer, Sir Edwin	*Dignity and Impudence* 58
Lobel, Arnold	"George the Cat" 126
Magritte, René	*Time Transfixed* 115
Marin, John	*Cape, Split, and Boat* 47
	Circus Elephants 6
Matisse, Henri	*The Snail* 60
	The Abby Aldrich Rockefeller Memorial Window 52
Michelangelo	*Piéta* 51
Monet, Claude	*Beach at Trouville* 91
	The Seine at Lavacourt 67
Motte, Henri	*The Trojan Horse* 34
O'Gorman, Juan	*Library, National Autonomous University of Mexico* 101
O'Keeffe, Georgia	*Red Canna* 44
Picasso, Pablo	*Family of Saltimbanques* 22
	Girl Before a Mirror 62
	Head of a Young Man 32
	Mother and Child 6
Renoir, Pierre Auguste	*Monet Working in His Garden at Argenteuil* 40
Rickey, George	*Three Red Lines* 30
Rigaud, Hyacinthe	*Louis XV as a Child* 86
Rivera, Diego	*Flower Day* 102
Rousseau, Henri	*Equatorial Jungle* 36
	Sleeping Gypsy 12
Rubens, Peter Paul	*Lion* 18
Sargent, John Singer	*Muddy Alligators* 44
Schulz, Charles	*Peanuts* 130
Seurat, Georges	*Study for "La Grande Jatte"* 41
Silverstein, Shel	"Anteater" 127
Smith, Dennis	Fountain figure in bronze 15
Stella, Frank	*Sinjerli Variation 1* 52
Sultan, Donald	*Lemon, Jan. 17, 1984* 4
Thiebaud, Wayne	*Rabbit* 19
Tzu-Hsi	*Peonies and Cat Meowing at Pug Dog* 26
Vermeer, Jan	*The Artist in His Studio* 14

Index

A
Abstract art, 22, 24, 42, 60
Adams, Herbert
   Singing Boys, 84
Allen, Jesse
   The Banyon Tree, 24
Allston, Washington, 8
   Belshazzar's Left Hand, 8
Alphabets, 120
Altamira cave paintings, 20
Animals in art, 2, 3, 4, 18, 19, 20, 24, 26, 34, 35, 44, 46, 58, 59, 60, 64, 65, 78, 110, 113, 126, 127
   imaginary, 64, 65, 66
   portraits of, 19, 58
Anno, Mitsumasa, 120
   Anno's Alphabet, 120, 121
Appliqué, 70
Architects, 92, 96, 100, 128
Architecture, 92, 94, 95, 96, 97, 98, 100, 128
   Kasho Kumagi, Malaysia, 97
   Neuschwanstein Castle, Germany, 97
   Sand castle, California, 96
   St. Basil's Cathedral, Moscow, 96
   Taj Mahal, India, 98
   Teotihuacan ruins, Mexico, 103
Armatures, 66
Art
   abstract, 22, 24, 42, 60
   advertising, 122
   cartoon, 130
   Chinese, 26, 79, 120
   Cubist, 62
   Egyptian, 69
   Greek, 78, 84
   Impressionistic, 40, 67, 91
   Japanese, 26, 118
   kinetic, 30
   Mexican, 102
   mosaic, 76
   movements, 114
   museums, 72, 134
   nonobjective, 30, 31
   pre-Columbian, 78
   prehistoric, 20
   primitive, 12
   realistic, 30, 31, 62
   Renaissance, 50, 51
   representational, 22
   surrealistic, 114
Artists
   cartoonists, 130
   costume designers, 86
   graphic designers, 124
   illustrators, 126
   kinds of, 14
   styles of, 22, 60
Asymmetrical balance, 52
Asymmetrical design, 80
Aztec, 103

B
Background, 48, 116
Balance, 30, 52
   in mobiles, 31
Banners, 104
Bark cloth, 74
Bas relief, 84
Bleach, 7
Boccioni, Umberto, 38
   The City Rises, 39
Brayer, 29, 118, 119
Buildings,
   design of, 92, 101
   models of, 100

C
Calder, Alexander, 1, 30
   Camel drawing, 4
   Fish Mobile, 1
   Untitled (Mobile), 30
Calligraphy, 26

Camera, 132
Cartoon art, 130
Castles, 96
Cave paintings, 20, 58
Center of interest, 11, 29, 105
Chalk, colored, 18, 19, 21
Charcoal, 9
Chinese art, 26, 78, 120
    Li Po Chanting a Poem, 27
    Peonies and Cat Meowing at Pug Dog, 26
    Vase, 79
Circles, 12, 52, 53
Circular weaving, 72, 73
Clay, 54, 80, 81
Closed shapes, 6
Cloth, 70, 86
Clothing design, 86
Cohoon, Hannah
    The Tree of Light or *Blazing Tree,* 25
Coil method, clay, 80
Collage, 14, 15, 108
Colosseum, 94, 95
Column of Independence, 98, 99
Colors
    analogous, 105
    complementary, 36, 37, 38, 40, 105, 116
    dominant, 38
    earth, 20
    in graphic design, 122
    intensity of, 36
    mixing, 22, 23, 36, 37
    monochrome, 106
    neutral, 36
    optical mixing of, 40
    primary, 38, 46
    relationships, 38
Color scheme, 38
Color wheel, 36, 37
Comic strips, 130, 131
Compass, 53, 128
Complementary colors, 36, 37, 38, 40, 105, 116
    split complements of, 38
    traids of, 38
Composition, 10, 11, 15, 28, 46, 132
    foreground in, 26
    in graphic design, 122
Computer generated image of DNA, 52

Contour drawing, 4, 5, 6
Contrast, 19
Costumes, 86, 87
Cubism, 62
Cuna Indians, 70
Currier, Nathaniel
    The Road—Winter, 119
Cutouts, 60, 61, 71

D
Dali, Salvador, 114
    The Persistence of Memory, 114
Da Vinci, Leonardo, 50
    Mona Lisa, 50
Degas, Edgar, 82
    Ballerina, 82
Delaunay, Robert
    Political Drama, 23
Depth, 8, 12, 19, 48, 90
Design, 14
    architectural, 96
    clothing, 86
    container, 78, 80
    creating a radial, 53
    geometric, 74, 75
    graphic, 122, 124
    Oriental, 26
    printmaking and, 28
    Shaker, 24
Designing
    an alphabet, 121, 122
    on bark cloth, 74, 75
    a costume, 87
    containers, 78, 108
    a greeting card, 124, 125
    an imaginary beast, 64, 65, 66
    a label, 122, 123
    medals, 54, 55
    pendants, 54
    prints, 119
    a treasure box, 108, 109
Diorama, 100
Distance, showing, 26, 48, 90, 91
Distortion, 62, 114
Doric architecture, 94
Drawing
    animals, 3, 19
    basic shapes, 12, 13
    with bleach, 7

buildings, 92, 93, 95, 96, 97, 99
contour, 4, 5, 6
a fantasy tree, 24
human figure, the 83, 85
lines, 2, 3, 4, 5
mass, 6
mechanical, 128
from memory, 16
portraits, 32
a self-portrait, 107
textures, 2, 3
trees, 25
with a viewfinder, 11
Dufy, Raoul, 33
Le Haras du Pin, 33
Dürer, Albrecht, 2, 50
Rhinoceros, 2
Young Woman in Netherlandish Dress 51

E
Eakins, Thomas, 56
Max Schmidt in a Single Scull, 56
Earth colors, 20, 21
Edison, Thomas, 132
Egyptian art, 68, 69
King Tut mask, 69
Offering Bearer, 69
Sphinx of Amenhotep III, 69
Egyptians and weaving, 72
El Greco, 48
View of Toledo, 49
Emphasis, 11, 29, 92, 112, 114
Empty shapes, 6
Escher, M. C., 110, 111, 112, 113
Drawing Hands, 112
Relativity, 113
Sky and Water I, 110, 112
Exteriors, 90

F
Fantasy and art, 64, 66, 114
Fiber art, 72
Film, 132
Fingerprints, 28
Flags, 104
Foil relief, 92
Foreground, 11, 26, 48
Forms, 12, 14, 19, 67

Freeman, Nancy, 70
The Fish Market, 70

G
Gadzala, Virginia,
Prince Serpuhofsky, 87
Gypsy, 87
Gainsborough, Thomas, 10
Landscape with a Bridge, 10
Galleries, 72, 134
Gauguin, Paul, 38
Woman with Mango, 38
Geometric shapes, 12, 19, 74
Gerard, Jean, 110
Gericault, Theodore, 35
Horse Race at the Start, 35
Gradation, 8, 18, 45
Grandeville, 110
Heads of Men and Animals Compared, 110
Graphic design, 122, 124
Greek architecture, 94
Greek art, 78, 84
Vase, 78
Greeting card designs, 124

H
Harnett, William, 56
My Gems, 57
Hassam, Childe, 90
Boston Common at Twilight, 90
Highlighting and shading, 8, 18, 120
Hiroshige, Utagawa, 118
Travelers at Shono in Heavy Rain, 118
Hokusai
Tuning the Samisen, 27
Holbien III, Hans, 54
Henry VIII, 54
Holmquist, Anders, 104
Wings, 104
Homer, Winslow, 46, 56
Mink Pond, 46
Snap the Whip, 57
Horizon line, 48, 90, 115
Horizontal, 10, 48
Human figure, 82
drawing the, 83, 85
Hurd Peter, 48
Eve of St. John, 48

I
Ideograms, 120
Illusion, 110, 112, 113, 116
    Persian, *Four Horses Concentric Design,* 113
    Illustrated alphabets, 120
    Illustrations, 120, 126, 128
    Imagination and art, 10, 16, 64, 66, 110
    Impressionism, 40

J
Japanese art, 26, 27, 118
    Travelers at Shono in Heavy Rain, 118
    Tuning the Samisen, 27

K
Kiln, 55, 81
Kinetic art, 30

L
Landscapes, 10, 24
    Surrealistic, 114, 115
Landseer, Sir Edwin, 58, 59
    Dignity and Impudence, 58
Lascaux cave paintings, 20, 21
Lettering, 125
Light
    use of, 67
    values of, 8
Lines, 2, 4, 14, 26, 28, 42, 96
    in calligraphy, 26
    outlines, 5
Lobel, Anita, 126
Lobel, Arnold, 126
    "George the Cat", 126

M
Magritte, René, 114
    Time Transfixed, 115
Manhole covers, 135
Marin, John, 6, 46
    Cape, Split, and Boat, 47
    Circus Elephants, 6
Marionettes, 88
Mask, paper, in drawing, 5
Mass, 6, 10
Materials, art, 76, 83
Matisse, Henri, 52, 60
    The Snail, 60
    The Abby Aldrich Rockefeller Memorial Window, 52
Mayan Indians, Mexico, 103
McGregor, LaRene
    Circle weaving, 72
Mechanical drawing, 128
Medallions, 54
Media, artists', 76, 83
Mexican art, 102, 103
Michelangelo Buonarroti, 50
    Pieta, 51
Middle ground, 48
Mobiles, 30, 31
Models, 92, 100
Molas, 70
Monet, Claude, 90
    Beach at Trouville, 91
    Seine at Lavacourt, The, 67
Monuments, 98, 99
Moods, creating a mood, 24, 42, 60
Moore, Lynne, 118
Mosaics, 76
    Court of Justinian, 76
Motion pictures, 132
Motte, Henri
    The Trojan Horse, 34
Movement, creating, 47, 132, 135
Movies, 132
Murals, 83
Museums, 71, 132
Myths, illustrating, 77

N
Natural objects, printmaking with, 28, 29
Nonobjective art, 30, 60

O
O'Gorman, Juan, 101
    Library mosaic, National Autonomous University of Mexico, 101
Oil pastels, 18, 19
O'Keeffe, Georgia, 44
    Red Canna, 44
Open shapes, 6
Optical mixing, 40
Oriental art, 26, 76, 78, 118, 120
Outlines, 4, 5
Ovals, 12, 18
Overlapping, 37, 90

P

Paint, 20
   kinds of, 44
   mixing, 22, 23
   tempera, 37
   watercolors, 44, 46
Painting
   animals, 58
   with earth colors, 21
   imaginary beasts, 65
   Impressionistic, 40, 41
   landscapes, 10
   to music, 42
   Oriental, 26, 27
   portraits, 10
   still lifes, 39, 56, 57
   with tempera, 37
   with watercolors, 44, 45, 46
   waterscapes, 46, 47
Papier-mâché, 66
Parthenon, 94
Patterns, 2, 4, 12, 28, 42, 70, 72, 86
Pencil shading, 9
Perception, 112, 113
Perspective, one-point, 90
Picasso, Pablo, 6, 62
   Family of Saltimbanques, 22
   Girl Before a Mirror, 62
   Head of a Young Man, 32
   Mother and Child, 7
Pioneer Handcart monument, 99
Planes, in kinetic sculpture, 30
Poem illustrations, 126, 127
Pointillism, 40
Portraits, 32, 86, 106
   of animals, 58
   drawing, 63
   self-portraits, 106
   two-view, 62, 63
Pottery, 80
   clay coil method, 80, 81
Pre-Columbian art, 78
Primitive art, 12
Printmaking, 28, 29, 118
Prints, 2, 28, 29, 118, 119
Profiles in portraits, 62, 63
Proportion, 18, 50, 58, 82, 84, 106
Puppets, 88
Puzzles, 112, 113, 116

R

Realism, 2, 50, 56, 58, 114
Relief foil, 92
Relief prints, 118
Relief sculptures, 84
Renaissance, 50
Renoir, Pierre August, 40
   Monet Painting in His Garden at Argenteuil, 40
Representational art, 22
Reverse appliqué, 70
Rhino Wolf, 64
Rhythm, 42, 47
Rickey, George, 30
   Three Red Lines, 30
Rigaud, Hyacinth, 86
   Louis XV as a Child, 86
Rivera, Diego, 102
   Flower Day, 102
Roman architecture, 94, 95
Roundness, in shading, 8, 9
Rousseau, Henri, 12
   The Equatorial Jungle, 36
   The Sleeping Gypsy, 12
Rubens, Peter Paul, 18
   Lion, 18
Rule of compensation, 10

S

Sargent, John Singer, 44
   Muddy Alligators, 44
Schulz, Charles
   Peanuts, 130
Scoring, clay, 81
Sculpture
   kinetic, 30
   medal, 54
   mobile, 30
   papier–mâché, 66
   relief, 54, 84
   stabile, 30
Seascapes, 46, 114
Self-portrait, monochrome, 106
Seurat, Georges, 40
   Study for "La Grande Jatte", 41
Shading, 2, 8, 16, 17, 18, 22, 112
Shaker design, 24
Shapes, 2, 4, 6, 14, 18, 19, 42, 52, 61, 112, 116

geometric, 12, 19, 74
three-dimensional, 12
two-dimensional, 12
Silhouettes, 86
Silverstein, Shel, 126
"Anteater", 127
Slip, clay, 81
Smith, Dennis
Fountain figure in bronze, 15
Space, 14, 28, 90, 110, 112, 116
negative, 110, 116
positive, 110, 116
Split complements, 38
Stabile, 30
Stained glass, 52
Stella, Frank, 52
Sinjerli Variation 1, 52
Still life, 39, 56, 57
Storyboards, 132, 133
Sultan, Donald
Lemon, Jan 17, 1984, 4
Surrealism, 114
Symbols, 74, 75, 99, 101, 104, 135
Symmetrical design, 80
Symmetry, 24, 46, 80, 94

T
T square, 128
Taj Majal, 98
Tapa cloth, 74
Technical drawing, 128
Tempera, 37
Tesserae, 76
Texture, 2, 3, 4, 14, 42
and clay, 81
drawing, 17, 18, 25

in printmaking, 28
using values to create, 8
in watercolor painting, 45
Thiebaud, Wayne, 18
Rabbit, 19
Tints, 22, 23
Toltec Indians, Mexico, 103
Tones, 22, 23, 46
Topography, 48
Trees, 24
Towers, 96, 97
Transformations, 110, 111
Turrets, 96, 97
Tzu-Hsi
Peonies and Cat Meowing at Pug Dog, 26

U
Unity, 25, 99
Unicorn, 64
Universal symbols, 74, 75

V
Values, light and dark, 8, 14, 25
Value scale, constructing a, 8, 9
Vanishing point, 90
Vermeer, Jan
The Artist in His Studio, 14
Vexillography, 104
Viewfinder, 10, 11

W
Wash, watercolor, 45
Watercolors, 44, 46
Waterscapes, 46
Weaving, 72, 73

Acknowledgments

We gratefully acknowledge the valuable contributions of the following artists, consultants, editorial advisors, and reviewers who participated in the development of this book: Ruth Jones and C.J. Greenwald, teachers, St. Luke's Lutheran Day School, La Mesa, CA; Mirta Golino, art educator and editorial advisor, San Diego; Jeff Jurich, animator and writer, Celluloid Studios, Denver; Dennis Smith, sculptor, Highland, UT; Virginia Gadzala, costume designer, San Diego; Phyllis Thurston, former Art Supervisor, Pinellas County School District, Clearwater, FL; Judy Chicago and Mary Ross Taylor, Through the Flower, Benicia, CA; Andrew Blanks, Jr., art teacher, Johnston Middle School, Houston; Barbara Pearson Roberts, teacher, Sabal Palm Elementary School, Tallahassee; Shirley and Terry McManus, puppetry consultants, "Puppets Please," San Diego; Dr. Wayne Woodward, associate professor of art education, Georgia Southwestern College; Mary Riggs of Riggs Galleries, San Diego; Anna Ganahl, Director of Public Relations, Art Center College of Design, Pasadena; Francoise Gilot, artist, La Jolla, CA; Leven C. Leatherbury, independent consultant in art education, San Diego; Betty Cavanaugh, curriculum consultant in art education, Upland, CA; Joel Hagen, artist and writer, Oakdale, CA; Kellene Champlin, Art Supervisor, Fulton County Schools, Atlanta; Mar Gwen Land, art teacher, Montgomery Jr. High School, San Diego; LaRene McGregor, fiber artist, McKenzie Bridge, OR; Norma Wilson, former art teacher and editorial advisor, San Diego; Dr. Ann S. Richardson, Supervisor of Art, Foreign Languages, and Gifted and Talented Education, Charles County Public Schools, LaPlata, MD; Talli Larrick, educator and writer, El Cajon, California; Mary Apuli, Coordinator of Elementary Program, Indiana School District No. 16, Minneapolis; Carol Widdop-Sonka, artist and writer, San Diego; Virginia Fitzpatrick, art educator and writer, Bloomington, IN; Evelyn Ackerman, artist, Era Industries, Culver City, CA; Judy Kugel, teacher trainer for Learning to Read Through the Arts, New York City; Arlie Zolynas, educator and author, San Diego; Nancy Remington, Principal, Sacramento Country Day School, Sacramento; Kay Alexander, Art Consultant, Palo Alto School District, Palo Alto, CA; Billie Phillips, Lead Art Supervisor, St. Louis Public Schools, St. Louis; Sister Marie Albert, S.S.J., Principal, St. Callistus School, Philadelphia; Robert Vickrey, artist, Orleans, MA.

We especially appreciate the students from the following schools who contributed the student art reproduced in this series: O.H. Anderson Elem. School, Mahtomedi, MN; Atkinson Elem. School, Barnesville, MN; W.D. Hall Elem. School, El Cajon, CA; Idlewild Elem. School, Memphis, TN; Irving Elem. School, St. Louis, MO: MacArthur Elem. School, Indianapolis, IN; Oakwood Elem. School, Knoxville, TN; John Roe Elem. School, St. Louis, MO; Taylors Falls School District #140, Taylors Falls, MN; Washington Elem. School, Pamona, CA; Enterprise Elem. School, Enterprise, FL; Kellogg Elem. School, Chula Vista, CA; Learning to Read Through the Arts, New York, NY; Lewis School, San Diego; Woodcrest Elem. School, Fridley, MN; Westwood Elem. School, San Diego; Indep. School District #16, Minneapolis, MN; St. Luke's Lutheran Day School, La Mesa, CA; Country Day School, Sacramento, CA; Budd School, Fairmont, MN; Park Terrace Elem. School, Spring Lake Park, MN; Audubon Elem. School, Baton Rouge, LA; Chilowee Elem. School, Knoxville, TN; Logan Elem. School, San Diego; Grassy Creek Elem. School, Indianapolis, IN; Earle Brown Elem. School, Brooklyn Center, MN; Jefferson Elem. School, Winona, MN; Calvert Elem. School, Prince Frederick, MD; Barnsville Elem. School, Barnsville, MN; Ridgedale Elem. School, Knoxville, TN; Children's Creative and Performing Arts Academy, San Diego; Steven V. Correia School, San Diego; Walnut Park Elem. School, St. Louis, MO.

Although it is impossible to acknowledge all the contributors to this project, we express special thanks for the generous efforts of the following individuals: Janet Reim, Gail Kozar, Rae Murphy, Jan Thompson, Gerald Williams, Timothy Asfazadour, Judy Cannon, Helen Negley, Crystal Thorson, Rachelle and Tyler Bruford, Mary Bluhm, David Zielinski, David Oliver, Daniel and Carl Bohman, Anne G. Allen, Bao Vuong, Gail W. Guth, Signe Ringbloom, Claire Murphy, Joan Blaine, Patrice M. Sparks, and Larke Johnston.

Coronado Staff: Marsha Barrett Lippincott, Level 1 Editor; Janet Kylstad Coulon, Level 2 Editor; Deanne Kells Cordell, Level 3 Editor; Carol Spirkoff Prime, Level 4 Editor; Patricia McCambridge, Level 5 Editor; DeLynn Decker, Level 6 Editor; Janis Heppell, Project Designer; Lisa Peters, Designer; Myrtali Anagnostopoulos, Designer; Debra Saleny, Photo Research.